Cultivating Leadership in Early Childhood Education and Care fills a gap that ECE leaders are constantly lamenting. There is a dearth of leadership resources for emerging leaders and service leaders of early childhood education and care services. This book will be welcomed and is extremely useful with a mix of theory and practical applications for leaders in this field.

Su Garrett, *Director, Explore & Develop, Annandale*

This book examines the complexities of leadership in ECEC and bridges the gap between theory and practice. Readers are urged to create a learning culture within early childhood environments and to empower and inspire the leadership in all educators. For anyone who is interested in leading and learning more about what enables effective leadership in early childhood educational contexts this is a must read!

Dr Jo Grimmond, *University of Wollongong*

The author explores the challenges that traditional leadership paradigms have raised within the ECEC profession and offers a path forward through reframing leadership development, knowledge and skills. This book offers an optimistic vision for the future of leadership in early childhood education. I highly recommend this book to anyone passionate about driving positive organisational change through leadership but particularly for established and emerging leaders in the early childhood profession.

Dr Belinda Downey, *Charles Sturt University*

In the important but complex and demanding space of early childhood education and care (ECEC) developing and nurturing leadership is essential to achieving positive outcomes for children and families and for educator well-being. Leanne Gibbs in her book "Cultivating Leadership in Early Childhood Education and Care: Trouble, Complexity and Promise" provides a realistic insight into the challenges of cultivating leadership in ECEC along with a compelling and inspiring alternative approach to leadership development. Through the sharing of leadership stories Leanne highlights practices that enable the development of effective leadership. This book will encourage you to think deeply about the definition, practice, and development of leadership in ECEC and inspire educators who are on a leadership journey!

Marina Papic, *Professor of Early Childhood Education, Australian Catholic University*

Cultivating Leadership in Early Childhood Education and Care

This book redefines leadership in early childhood education (ECE), offering fresh theoretical insights and practical approaches.

Delving into the challenges of the workforce in the ECE sector, this book unravels the narrative of leadership development. It underscores the importance of leadership practices in maintaining process quality within ECE, which significantly impacts children's academic, emotional and social outcomes and life trajectories. The book presents novel conceptualisations of leadership, shedding light on factors that enable and constrain leadership development through the theoretical frameworks of complexity leadership theory and the theory of practice architectures. It also provides practical strategies for cultivating leadership within early childhood organisations. Through interviews and case studies, the book brings to life the experiences of ECE leaders, amplifying important themes and experiences.

This book is an invaluable read for educators and leaders around the world, providing inspiration and guidance for their leadership journey. It is also an empirically based must-read for lecturers and students in the higher education sector.

Dr **Leanne Gibbs** is Senior Lecturer at Charles Sturt University. She joined Charles Sturt University after an exemplary career within Australian early childhood education. Her research interests include leadership, advocacy and public policy, and she has published extensively on the topic of leadership emergence and cultivation in early childhood education.

Cultivating Leadership in Early Childhood Education and Care

Trouble, Complexity and Promise

Leanne Gibbs

Routledge
Taylor & Francis Group

LONDON AND NEW YORK

Designed cover image: © Getty Images

First published 2025
by Routledge
4 Park Square, Milton Park, Abingdon, Oxon OX14 4RN

and by Routledge
605 Third Avenue, New York, NY 10158

Routledge is an imprint of the Taylor & Francis Group, an informa business

© 2025 Leanne Gibbs

The right of Leanne Gibbs to be identified as author of this work has been asserted in accordance with sections 77 and 78 of the Copyright, Designs and Patents Act 1988.

All rights reserved. No part of this book may be reprinted or reproduced or utilised in any form or by any electronic, mechanical, or other means, now known or hereafter invented, including photocopying and recording, or in any information storage or retrieval system, without permission in writing from the publishers.

Trademark notice: Product or corporate names may be trademarks or registered trademarks, and are used only for identification and explanation without intent to infringe.

British Library Cataloguing-in-Publication Data
A catalogue record for this book is available from the British Library

Library of Congress Cataloging-in-Publication Data
Names: Gibbs, Leanne, author.
Title: Cultivating leadership in early childhood education and care : trouble, complexity and promise / Leanne Gibbs.
Description: Abingdon, Oxon ; New York, NY : Routledge, 2025. | Includes bibliographical references and index.
Identifiers: LCCN 2024026640 (print) | LCCN 2024026641 (ebook) | ISBN 9781032234373 (hardback) | ISBN 9781032234366 (paperback) | ISBN 9781003277590 (ebook)
Subjects: LCSH: Early childhood education--Administration. | Educational leadership.
Classification: LCC LB2822.6 .G53 2025 (print) | LCC LB2822.6 (ebook) | DDC 372.12--dc23/eng/20240620
LC record available at https://lccn.loc.gov/2024026640
LC ebook record available at https://lccn.loc.gov/2024026641

ISBN: 978-1-032-23437-3 (hbk)
ISBN: 978-1-032-23436-6 (pbk)
ISBN: 978-1-003-27759-0 (ebk)

DOI: 10.4324/9781003277590

Typeset in Optima
by SPi Technologies India Pvt Ltd (Straive)

This book is dedicated to all who lead early childhood education and care across the world especially and to Professor Manjula Waniganayake.

Contents

List of Illustrations x
Acknowledgements xi
Glossary xii

Prologue 1

PART I TROUBLE 11

1 We Need to Talk About Leadership in ECEC 13
2 Thinking Differently About Leadership Theory and Practice 34

PART II COMPLEXITY 55

3 Dispositions for Leading: Knowledge, Skills, Values 57
4 The Complex Site of ECEC: Where Leadership Happens 79

PART III PROMISE 103

5 Organisations Cultivating and Shaping Leadership 105
6 Learning for Leading 126
7 A Path Ahead 147

Appendix: Research Studies 160
Index 171

Illustrations

Figures

Figure 0.1 The influence of effective leadership within
early childhood education 2
Figure 1.1 Leadership in early childhood education 13
Figure 2.1 An analysis of leaders' data through the CLT lens 44
Figure 4.1 The sites of ECEC 86
Figure 4.2 The education complex in ECEC (Salamon et al.,
2024). Adapted from Kemmis et al. (2012) 88
Figure 6.1 Framework for professional learning for leading 136

Tables

Table 3.1 Self-perception of knowledge, skills and values (Study 2) 65
Table 5.1 Leadership Observation Tool for observation of
practices that support the emergence and
development of leadership 119
Table 5.2 Questions for reflection 122
Table A.1 Study 1 participants 161
Table A.2 Leadership Observation Tool 163
Table A.3 Study 2 participants 166

# Acknowledgements

I wish to acknowledge and thank all research participants who so generously gave their time, perspectives and stories in the interest of advancing the early childhood education and care profession and leadership in the field. Thank you also to my doctoral supervisors, Professor Frances Press, Professor Sandie Wong and Dr Tamara Cumming, and my colleagues who have helped to shape my ideas and thinking.

Glossary

Early childhood education and care (ECEC) settings refer to environments where young children, typically from birth to school age, receive education and care. These settings embody social, physical, emotional, personal, creative and cognitive learning and development for children. Qualified and experienced educators deliver education and care through learning frameworks and a pedagogy of education and care. The structure and organisation of ECEC settings vary worldwide, reflecting different cultural, societal and governmental contexts. However, the common goal is to ensure children's health, safety, well-being and educational outcomes. These settings are crucial in shaping a child's early development and preparing them for their future educational journey.

Acronyms

ECEC early childhood education and care
ECT   early childhood teacher
CAS   complex adaptive systems
CLT   complexity leadership theory

Prologue

> *Organisations need to offer genuine opportunities for growth and leadership, and the journey needs to be fostered with regularity and purpose. Any support for leadership development needs time allocated so that skills, ideas and scenarios can be fleshed out. Educators need encouragement and appropriate challenge from their leaders; they need their leaders to walk side-by-side with them across known and unknown territories.*
>
> —Shannon, Study 1

Why this book, now?

Now is a unique time and circumstance to highlight recent innovative and creative empirical research and standpoints on leadership cultivation and practice. With significant agreement on the influence of leadership on the quality of early childhood education and care (ECEC), it is timely to understand how leadership emerges and develops. This book shares stories of leadership, and the intention is to change perspectives and thinking away from individualistic, centralised leadership to leadership that is a practice open to many within the ECEC profession. More must be done to cultivate and inspire leadership in ECEC to benefit children, their families and the global community.

Leadership is critical in ECEC. Evidence shows an association between effective leadership and process quality within ECEC and positive outcomes for educator well-being. Further, international ECEC workforce strategies

DOI: 10.4324/9781003277590-1

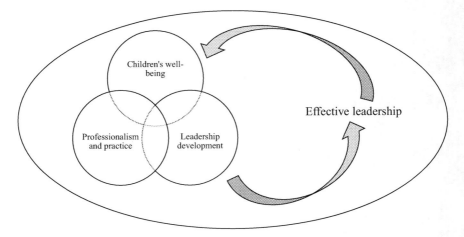

Figure 0.1 The influence of effective leadership within early childhood education.

highlight that cultivating effective leadership as a pathway to workforce sustainability is a key challenge for the ECEC profession (Douglass, 2019).

There are, therefore, compelling reasons for a book on the development of effective leadership within early childhood education (ECE). First, effective leadership within ECEC favourably affects children's well-being (Douglass, 2019; Harrison et al., 2020; McCoy et al., 2017). Second, effective leadership inspires communities of educators and shapes their professionalism and practice (Brooker & Cumming, 2019; McKinlay et al., 2018). Third, new leaders are shaped by existing leaders who create the conditions for the emergence and development of leadership (Douglass, 2018; Wilkinson, 2017). These three elements influence and interact, continually change and adapt to the conditions around them and generate the conditions for leadership development (Uhl-Bien & Marion, 2009). Figure 0.1 demonstrates these relationships.

Children's well-being

Leadership within early childhood sites influences the quality and effectiveness of education for young children (Douglass, 2019; Harrison et al., 2020; McCoy et al., 2017). Further, studies have shown that specific practices of leadership are enacted within high-quality ECEC settings. These practices include engaging responsively with families, using evidence to drive improvements in outcomes, being strategic, facilitating open communication, embracing integrated working, motivating and empowering staff, and being committed to their own and others' learning (Coleman et al., 2016; Siraj-Blatchford & Manni, 2007).

Professionalism and practice

The practices of positional leaders and organisations influence the experience and longevity of educators in ECEC (Brooker & Cumming, 2019; Irvine et al., 2016; McKinlay et al., 2018). Some challenges inhibit the development of a knowledgeable and skilled workforce. These challenges include the lack of preparation for leadership within ECEC. They could lead to an inadequate leadership pipeline from within the sector and may, therefore, result in a loss of ECE orientation to leading and developing the field (Nicholson & Kroll, 2015).

Developing effective leaders

Leadership scholarship is continually developing, and leadership efficacy depends upon knowledge of theory and practice, critical reflection and a sustainable development pathway for emerging leaders (Nicholson & Kroll, 2015). However, leadership cultivation focuses predominantly on individuals within positional roles; thus, it limits the development of leading as a practice. The emergence of leadership and the everyday practice of leadership may, therefore, be overlooked (Lichtenstein et al., 2006).

Cultivating early childhood leadership: Trouble, complexity and promise challenges prevailing thought on leadership in many contexts but particularly in the ECEC profession. This book shines a light on cultivating leadership. The unique phenomena of leadership emergence and development in ECEC and leaders' unique dispositions are worthy of in-depth exploration. By reading this book, organisations and positional and emerging leaders will engage with the leadership development story and understand new ways of cultivating leading and leadership.

With this book, I want to disrupt current thinking on persistent issues and challenges in leadership conceptualisation and development. By sharing contemporary stories of leading and leadership, I hope to inspire and influence organisational action.

Overview of the book

The book is divided into three parts. *Part I: Trouble* outlines the origins of leadership in ECEC and the challenges it faces to ongoing development and conceptualisations and theoretical perspectives on leadership. *Part II: Complexity* illuminates the complex site of ECEC organisations where leadership happens and the diverse knowledge, skills and values of emerging and positional leaders. *Part III: Promise* explores the possibilities and innovative approaches for the development of leaders and the practice of leading. Part III also lays out an optimistic path for leadership in ECEC, a critical issue for the ECEC sector and, subsequently, for children's outcomes and civil society.

Each chapter begins with an overview of chapter content. Chapter content is explored and explained, and descriptive stories from research are shared. Chapters conclude with a series of questions and a suggested activity for reflection and action.

Part I — Trouble: difficulty, problem

Chapter 1: We need to talk about leadership in ECEC

Chapter 1 is an introduction to the ECEC leadership story. Historical perspectives, theories and practices are explored, and this provides insight into the current state of leadership in ECEC. Familiar themes such as the leadership and management dichotomy, pedagogical and operational leadership confluence and leadership as a practice or a position are examined. The themes are set within the international context. The challenges to leadership cultivation and development are elucidated.

Chapter 2: Thinking differently about leadership theory and practice

Leadership theories and conceptualisations are explored in Chapter 2. These theories and conceptualisations are placed in the current context and build on the work of scholars such as Rodd (2013), Stamopoulos and Barblett (2018) and Waniganayake et al. (2023). Theoretical accounts include complexity leadership theory, complex adaptive systems and practice theories. The chapter describes conceptualisations, including that of leading being a practice occurring as a relational activity with collective approaches that share the responsibility of the educational development of children and educators rather than achieving organisational goals (Wilkinson, 2017).

Prologue

Part II — Complexity: the state of being complex, complicated, interrelated parts

Chapter 3: Skills, knowledge and values: What do leaders look like?

Chapter 3 explores persistent questions about what leaders 'look' like and what knowledge, skills and values are both present and essential for emerging and positional leaders within ECEC. This chapter also discusses disconnection issues in the leadership story, specifically what educators consider a 'good' leader and what a 'good' leader really is. Leader profiles and stories are embedded within this chapter.

Chapter 4: The complex site of ECEC: Where leadership happens

Chapter 4 considers the complexity of ECEC organisations. ECEC, as a dynamic and multifaceted field, involves diverse stakeholders, contexts and goals. Organisations are not static nor isolated entities but complex sites that interact with their internal and external environments, and they evolve over time. This chapter explores ECEC as complex and adaptive systems and the concept of the 'education complex'. By using the lens of the education complex, ECEC leaders can critically reflect on the field and address the challenges and opportunities that ECEC leaders face in navigating the complexity of their work.

Part III — Promise: the quality of potential excellence to assure someone that one will definitely do something or that something will happen

Chapter 5: Organisations cultivating and shaping leadership

Chapter 5 positions the cultivation of leadership as an organisational responsibility from the human perspective and as an intentional consequence of other organisational arrangements. The term 'arrangements' refers to the conditions that shape the unfolding practices of leadership. According to Kemmis et al. (2014), there are three kinds of arrangements found within a site that shape practices: the cultural-discursive (evident in culture and language), the material-economic (evident in the physical spaces and material resources) and the social-political arrangements (evident in relationships and power).

This chapter is presented in three 'acts' that explore the elements of organisational culture and language, material resources and social-political

5

conditions and arrangements that build leadership from the ground up. The power of emerging and positional leaders to shape high-quality ECEC settings and to advocate for children, families and the community is illuminated. This chapter places the leadership development story firmly in the hands of ECEC organisations and disavows the narrative of the individual, charismatic, all-knowing leader.

Chapter 6: Learning for leading

Professional learning has the potential to send emerging and positional leaders on a transformative journey. This chapter delves into the many aspects of professional development by examining how it equips leaders with the knowledge, skills and reflective capacities crucial for navigating the complexities of the contemporary ECEC landscape. By fostering a culture of continuous learning, ECEC organisations have the potential to respond to the evolving context through effective leadership.

Through an exploration of professional learning practices and illuminating stories, this chapter highlights the intrinsic link between comprehensive and innovative professional learning and the cultivation and development of effective leadership.

Chapter 7: The path ahead for leadership in ECEC

The concluding chapter draws this in-depth exploration of leadership emergence and development to a close, highlighting the key concepts and ideas. The view ahead for early childhood leadership is evaluated through an optimistic and forward-thinking lens.

The three studies of leadership

This book is founded on contemporary theory and conceptualisations of expert opinions and perspectives from empirical studies, specifically three primary studies that analysed the emergence and development of leadership.

The three studies

These studies focused on leadership emergence and development in ECEC organisations. The research questions encompassed how emerging and

Prologue

positional leaders conceptualise and define 'leadership'. What skills, knowledge, values and dispositions are critical for ECEC leadership emergence and development? How do organisations cultivate and shape leadership through cultural-discursive, material-economic and social-political arrangements? What innovative practices create the conditions for leadership emergence and development?

The outcomes of all three studies include

- the identification of the organisational practices that enable and constrain the emergence and development of effective leading and leadership in early childhood organisations
- the identification of skills, knowledge, values and dispositions present in emerging and positional leaders across the world
- the recognition of innovative practices within ECEC organisations that enable leadership emergence and development and leading through challenging times

Study 1: A study of practices enabling the emergence and development of leading within exemplary Australian ECEC sites

The study (Gibbs, 2021) explored the challenges and initiatives of cultivating leadership in ECEC and proposed innovative approaches for fostering and developing leadership within ECEC organisations.

The research investigated emerging and positional leadership and its development in three ECEC settings in Australia, involving 24 participants. The study used complexity leadership theory as the ontological framework within complex adaptive systems to scrutinise patterns of emergence, interactions and unexpected outcomes.

The research involved a mini-ethnographic case study, which encompassed observing practices, unstructured interviews and dialogic cafés.

Study 2: A study of the emergence and development of leadership

This participatory, qualitative study engaged participants in conversations about the emergence and cultivation of leadership within ECEC. The conversations comprised appreciative inquiry and professional development founded on readings and provocations. The dynamic and emergent approach acknowledged the complexity of ECEC and elicited rich, complex outcomes.

Cultivating Leadership in Early Childhood Education and Care

Study 3: Leadership in early childhood organisations

The purpose of this research was to understand how a particular Australian ECEC organisation fostered and supported the workforce[1]. The study contributed to a conversation about the importance of leadership in ECEC as an influence on quality. It also added to the research showing that leadership is a concern for an organisation interested in preparing itself for the future; it must consider the development of workforce, leadership and innovation. The project investigated the experience and perceptions of over 500 employees, based in both ECEC settings and offices, on the development of leadership, innovation and workforce.

A case study methodology was used for this study, and the methods were diverse. Surveys, semi-structured interviews, reflective inquiry, focus groups, dialogic cafés and content analysis captured the voices of participants and structures of the organisation.

The stories and conversations in this book are drawn from these three studies. The emerging and positional leaders from these studies are also briefly profiled at the conclusion of this book.

Conclusion

This book is for anyone interested in leading and leadership, but it has particular salience for those interested in leadership within ECEC. The arguments within assert that there are alternative approaches to leadership that go beyond charismatic, individualistic and centralised leaders. The leadership story is open to the many rather than the few.

This book is not intended to be the definitive word on leadership or the practice of leading, particularly in ECEC settings, but it is intended to inspire effective leadership, new ways of leading and cultivating leadership, and the application of theory in practice.

This book is for all emerging and positional leaders who want to think and act in ways that disrupt the myth of the leader who is and does it all.

Note

1 Only the themes of this study are included. No participants are quoted.

References

Brooker, M. & Cumming, T. (2019). The 'dark side' of leadership in early childhood education. *Australasian Journal of Early Childhood*, 44(2), 111–123. https://doi.org/10.1177/1836939119832073

Coleman, A., Sharp, C. & Handscomb, G. (2016). Leading highly performing children's centres: Supporting development of the 'accidental leaders'. *Educational Management Administration & Leadership*, 44(5), 775–793. https://doi.org/10.1177/1741143215574506

Douglass, A. (2018). Redefining leadership: Lessons from an early education leadership development initiative. *Early Childhood Education Journal*, 46(4), 387–396. https://doi.org/10.1007/s10643-017-0871-9

Douglass, A. (2019). Leadership for quality early childhood education and care. *OECD Education Working Paper* (No. 211). OECD Publishing. https://doi.org/10.1787/6e563bae-en

Gibbs, L. (2021). A study of practices enabling the emergence and development of leading within exemplary Australian early childhood education sites [Doctoral thesis, Charles Sturt University]. Charles Sturt University. https://researchoutput.csu.edu.au/en/publications/a-study-of-practices-enabling-the-emergence-and-development-of-le

Harrison, L., Hadley, H., Irvine, I., Davis, B., Barblett, L., Hatzigianni, M. & Li, R. (2020). *Quality improvement research project*. Macquarie University and the Australian Children's Education & Care Quality Authority. https://www.acecqa.gov.au/resources/research#QIR, https://www.acecqa.gov.au/sites/default/files/2020-05/quality-improvement-research-project-2019.PDF

Irvine, S. L., Thorpe, K. J., McDonald, P., Lunn, J. & Sumsion, J. (2016). *Money, love and identity: Initial findings from the National ECEC Workforce study* [Summary report from the national ECEC Workforce Development Policy Workshop, Brisbane, Queensland]. Queensland University of Technology. https://eprints.qut.edu.au/101622/1/Brief_report_ECEC_Workforce_Development_Policy_Workshop_final.pdf

Kemmis, S., Wilkinson, J., Edwards-Groves, C., Hardy, I., Grootenboer, P. & Bristol, L. (2014). *Changing practices, changing education*. Springer.

Lichtenstein, B., Dooley, K. & Lumpkin, G. (2006). Measuring emergence in the dynamics of new venture creation. *Journal of Business Venturing*, 21(2), 153–175. https://doi.org/10.1016/j.jbusvent.2005.04.002

McCoy, D. C., Yoshikawa, H., Ziol-Guest, K. M., Duncan, G. J., Schindler, H. S., Magnuson, K. & Shonkoff, J. P. (2017). Impacts of early childhood education on medium-and long-term educational outcomes. *Educational Researcher*, 46(8), 474–487. https://doi.org/10.3102/0013189x17737739

McKinlay, S., Irvine, S. & Farrell, A. (2018). What keeps early childhood teachers working in long day care? Tackling the crisis for Australia's reform agenda in early childhood education and care. *Australasian Journal of Early Childhood*, 43(2), 32–42. https://doi.org/10.23965/ajec.43.2.04

Nicholson, J. & Kroll, L. (2015). Developing leadership for early childhood professionals through oral inquiry: Strengthening equity through making particulars visible in dilemmas of practice. *Early Child Development and Care, 185*(1), 17–43. https://doi.org/10.1080/03004430.2014.903939

Rodd, J. (2013). *Leadership in early childhood: the pathway to professionalism* (4th ed.). Allen & Unwin.

Siraj-Blatchford, I. & Manni, L. (2007). *Effective leadership in the early years sector: The ELEYS study*. Institute of Education, University of London.

Stamopoulos, E. & Barblett, L. (2018). *Early childhood leadership in action: Evidence-based approaches for effective practice*. Allen & Unwin.

Uhl-Bien, M. & Marion, R. (2009). Complexity leadership in bureaucratic forms of organizing: A meso model. *The Leadership Quarterly, 20*(4), 631–650. https://doi.org/10.1016/j.leaqua.2009.04.007

Waniganayake, M., Cheeseman, S., Fenech, M., Hadley, F. & Shepherd, W. (2023). *Leadership: Contexts and complexities in early childhood education* (3rd ed.). Oxford University Press.

Wilkinson, J. (2017). Leading as a socially just practice: Examining educational leading through a practice lens. In K. Mahon., S. Fransisco & S. Kemmis (Eds), *Exploring education and professional practice* (pp. 165–182). Springer.

PART 1

Trouble

Trouble: difficulty, problem

> Leadership ... I think it's a tough gig, responsibilities are huge, compliance is huge now, and I think some of those things have taken us away from children, the important stuff, and somehow we've got to find that balance.
>
> Passion, lifelong learning, qualifications, those qualities are really important, those qualities that you would want in a leader. I just don't mean caring and nurturing, but there are times when you need to have strength to deal with some really difficult situations.
>
> I think a good leader is knowing when to put up a hand and ask for help because it is sometimes lonely and thankless and a difficult job.
>
> —Ros, an education professional and leader for 40 years, Study 1

DOI: 10.4324/9781003277590-2

1 We Need to Talk About Leadership in ECEC

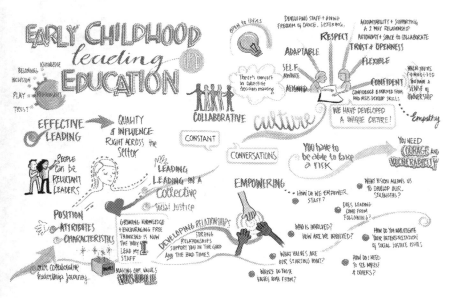

Figure 1.1 Leadership in early childhood education.

This chapter

- tells stories of leadership in ECEC
- explores the ECEC leadership origin story
- troubles the ECEC leadership narrative
- explains the challenges of leadership cultivation and development in ECEC.

DOI: 10.4324/9781003277590-3

A story of leadership

'It's like everyone tells a story about themselves inside their own head. Always. All the time. That story makes you what you are. We build ourselves out of that story.' –Rothfuss, 2010

> *I applied for the position of Director of a neighbourhood children's centre in the late 1980s—early in my career and on a whim. I am not sure what I was thinking. My career as an early childhood teacher had been a patchwork of epiphanies, joy and despair, and this was not a recommended pathway to a formal leadership role. But I wanted greater control over my professional experience. Despite my apparent weaknesses, the centre's Board of Management gave me the position. I was initiated into leadership practices within the early childhood education site.*
>
> *Memories of my early days in the role are fraught. I knew little about the enactment of leading—my pathway to leadership was unplanned. Although I held academic knowledge of children and their learning, I had no theoretical grounding in leadership. I was poorly prepared to take on the role. There were few formal opportunities for my development. At that time, I did not understand that my experience was typical of most emerging leaders in early childhood education.*
>
> *And so I was like a firefighting Alice in Wonderland—dousing spot fires and*
>
> > *chasing*
> > > *rabbits*
> > > > *down*
> > > > > *holes.*

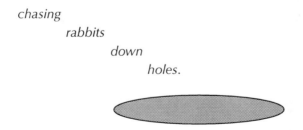

> *Following this initial challenge, I took on other leadership roles within the field. Leadership continued to be challenging. I stayed motivated by the potential of early childhood education to promote social and economic equality for children and families. The Perry Pre-school*

Project and subsequent research studies by Heckman (2011) and Sylva (2010) informed my view. These studies demonstrated the advantages of high-quality early childhood education for all children, particularly those experiencing disadvantage. I had first-hand experience with the impact of leadership on people, processes and organisations.

For 40 years, I have been confounded by leadership within ECEC [early childhood education and care]. Effective and sustainable leadership of ECEC teams, sites, organisations and the profession still seems complicated with overwhelming challenges, but I remain optimistic!

–Leanne

The single story but a common narrative

It is clear: the positional leader's skill and knowledge remain critical within the ECEC leadership story. Indeed, the quality of an ECEC setting is contingent on a positional leader's capacity to undertake a significant mission: maintain organisational harmony, demonstrate efficacy in administration, manage and deploy staff, know and understand policy and law, shape sophisticated educational programs, inspire, communicate a vision and develop others (Aubrey et al., 2013; Siraj-Blatchford & Manni, 2007). In this mission, the challenges and troubles for positional leaders are constant.

If effective leadership is pivotal in shaping the quality of ECEC, then nurturing the leadership abilities of both new and seasoned leaders is crucial. Leadership within ECEC transcends traditional roles, encompassing the collective knowledge, skills and values that empower educators to collaborate, drive innovation and champion the well-being of children and families.

There are at least three fundamental reasons why fostering leadership across all ECEC educators is vital. These reasons were introduced in the Prologue but are worthy of repetition. Firstly, it bolsters the professional identity and proficiency of educators, who often grapple with issues like inadequate compensation, high turnover and lack of acknowledgment. Leadership development equips educators to realise their ambitions and overcome challenges inherent in the ECEC profession by establishing a culture that values continuous learning, introspection and enhancement.

Secondly, leadership development significantly enhances the quality and effectiveness of ECEC methodologies, which rely on educators' adaptability to the diverse and evolving needs of children and families. By fostering a unified vision and shared principles, it promotes teamwork and dialogue among educators and other key participants, including parents, community figures and policymakers. Moreover, by encouraging ingenuity and forward thinking, it inspires educators to experiment with novel approaches and evaluate and refine their impact.

Lastly, it underpins the progression and representation of the ECEC sector, which frequently contends with challenges like underfunding, inadequate oversight, and marginalisation. Leadership development can transform public perception and the stance of policymakers by heightening the recognition of ECEC's significance and influence, thereby garnering support and resources for the field. It instils a sense of initiative and accountability, enabling educators to take part in and shape the policies and practices that govern ECEC.

Yet contemporary accounts from leaders continue to reflect the trials of leadership. Sally, an Australian early-childhood-setting leader, talks about the post-Covid-19 pandemic challenges of balancing the needs of all members of the ECEC community:

> *Like many others, I am feeling rather burnt out in guiding and managing staff at present. Our offering is high, yet we cannot compete with others in relation to wages. We offer a lovely place to work, exceptional ratios, great socials and so on. Since the pandemic, the expectations of some families are unachievable, and at times, staff feel undervalued for the important role they play. I love working with children, families and staff and have been in the sector a long time; however, being the employer of 40 staff and trying to meet everyone's needs is consistently difficult and can be very draining.*
>
> *–Sally, Study 2*

Marie gives this account of balancing administrative responsibilities:

> *Always busy ... NEVER enough time, even with one day in the office. My paid work hours are 8 am–4 pm Tues to Friday, but I work 'till 6 pm every day. Even on my office day, where there is no one else there, and I never ever have a lunch break. Just constantly busy trying to do jobs, and when all the 'to do' listed items*

We Need to Talk About Leadership in ECEC

are done, there's always another 'to do when you can' list that you start on. Heaps of emails that need tending, too. Official emails end up in junk mail, so I must continually scan this. I'm on several email groups and often get alerted through these of some funding or survey or training through the Dept of Education that must be done and that I've missed. There's 'never even read' weekly/ fortnightly emails from various advocacy and information organisations, including the Department of Education, that I just scan through now and file them in their email folder, as I know I will not get back to them to read through. I must prioritise this work and manage my time efficiently and effectively, or things don't get done even though I work [a] 10-hour day (and get paid for 8) every day. I never get everything done/finished or finished to my satisfaction. I am Nominated Supervisor / Early Childhood Teacher / Educational Leader. I have one office day a week, which is marvellous, but I have so many emails to go through and readings to do (that don't always get done), bureaucracy to troll through and manage, as well as families, staff and the teaching programme. I've been wanting to re-write the service philosophy since I started in March 2020 (as it is not great) but have not had the time. I've been wanting to create a Reconciliation Action Plan since March 2020, but, again, haven't had the time. We are working on beautifying our playground, and that is coming along, but little jobs, like painting the 'middle line' in our bike track, still isn't done—it's been on the list since March 2020!

—Marie, Study 2

The frustrations and complexity of the role of a leader are visible and continuing. Hence, the leadership narrative must change. The practice of leading, in its current form, is unsustainable, and educators are turning away from leadership. Yet the ECEC profession, now more than ever, needs more positional leaders and exemplary educators willing and skilled to lead. Therefore, the question of how leadership emerges, develops and is sustained must be explored in greater depth. The leadership origin story begins this exploration.

The ECEC leadership origin story

The evolution of ECEC programs in Europe and Anglo-American countries follows similar themes of child protection, education, inclusion of children with additional needs and enabling workforce participation, specifically women's participation. The path for the development of ECEC internationally starts from private charitable works and transforms into greater public responsibility in the early and middle 19th century. Public responsibility, particularly post World War II, encompassed two themes: care for poor and disadvantaged children of working mothers and the education and socialisation of children.

Pedagogical models for ECEC were predominantly short-day kindergartens (for education) and long-day nurseries (for care) founded on the theories of Friedrich Froebel, Johann Heinrich Pestalozzi and Maria Montessori (Kamerman & Gatenio-Gabel, 2007). There were, however, two key themes to the early development of ECEC in Europe: (1) protective services for neglected children and the children of poor working mothers and (2) preschool education focused on enhancing or enriching the development of middle-class children. After World War II, a third theme emerged in response to the needs of the growing numbers of women in the labour force who wanted decent quality and affordable care for their children.

In Australia, feminist philanthropic leaders established ECEC, just as others had worldwide, in the late 19th century. Embedding ECEC in legal and social reforms was foundational to children's progress and alleviating women's poverty (Brennan, 1998). Social justice concerns continued to drive the leadership for kindergarten and day care movements into the next century. In the early 20th century, advocacy for children and mothers resulted in the founding of kindergartens and day care centres. Kindergarten movements in Europe and America influenced Australian routines, teacher training and kindergarten operations.

ECEC transformed over the 20th century and was reshaped according to political and policy changes. Press and Hayes (2000) note that further ECEC development during this time transpired as initiatives for children's education, women's workforce participation and national economic improvement. Government jurisdictions, ideology and community sentiment influenced ECEC provision. These political and social arrangements established national and state systems encompassing centre-based preschool and long day care, family day care, occasional care and outside-of-school-hours care (Australian Government Department of Education, 2012; Press & Hayes, 2000).

The international development of ECEC has followed similar patterns and has been shaped by women's labour force participation, changes to family structures, where people live, inequality and a developing narrative of the importance of ECEC. The challenges of ECEC expansion across the world remain today—a lack of funding, complicated governance and jurisdictional structures, regional inequalities and ECEC workforce supply issues. Policy is fragmented and often split across multiple levels of government.

The context of leading in ECEC

The role of the ECEC leader has expanded internationally to include matters of regulatory compliance, staff development and developing educational programs and practices. For example, positional roles of ECEC leadership in Australia are mandated by law. Australian ECEC regulations require the positional roles of *approved provider, nominated supervisor* and *educational leader* to be formally appointed and to take on the legal responsibilities of managing and leading the administrative and educational operations of the ECEC setting (Australian Government Department of Education, 2012). These positions play an important role in the development of quality ECEC programs for children and families (Harrison et al., 2020).

Contrastingly, the Framework Plan for Kindergartens in Norway identifies two specific leadership roles in its ECEC centres: head teachers and pedagogical leaders. Those responsible for human resources, administration, organisational development and pedagogical practices are called head teachers. The pedagogical leader is involved in planning, implementing, documenting and assessing the children and the educational program and practice (Organisation for Economic Co-operation and Development [OECD], 2020).

Effective leadership, regardless of positional title, consists of many elements and interdependent components and is enacted within a constantly changing environment of policy, workforce precarity and child and family profiles (Gibbs et al., 2019). The sites of ECEC are, therefore, complex. Leadership enactment in such environments is also complex. (Chapter 4 discusses this in detail.)

The diverse nature of leadership within ECEC

Effective leadership influences positive outcomes for children's well-being, parents' workforce participation and economic growth in a mixed market environment (Alchin et al., 2019; Torii et al., 2017). In this environment, pedagogical and operational leaders play an important role in management, leadership and governance. In 2014, an Australian inquiry into 'childcare and early childhood learning' highlighted the complex range of skills required to lead in ECEC settings, including the capacity to deal with boards of directors, committees of management, funding mechanisms, industrial relations arrangements and the mentoring of staff, along with knowledge of child development and pedagogy (Australian Productivity Commission, 2014).

The complex nature of positional leadership roles is identified within international research, and the increasing complexity of a positional leadership role is concerning. Where more must be done to prepare leaders, the onus of facilitating leadership pathways for all educators falls to the positional leader (Douglass, 2019). Positional leaders in Australia must

> set strategic directions and foster professional values which inform how services operate. They promote a positive workplace culture which allows educators, coordinators and staff members to create and participate in collaborative and reflective learning communities. Positive workplace cultures support educators to learn from each other and develop professionally. Such workplaces welcome new ideas, encourage reflection and self-review, and motivate educators to pursue continuous improvement.
>
> (Australian Children's Education & Care Quality Authority, 2017, p. 5)

The over-reliance on the positional leaders to perform all these duties poses a risk to organisations and leaders themselves. This type of leadership, described as 'single-handed heroism' by Sinclair (2008, Loc. 199), is unsustainable and 'may be bad for leaders, followers and organisations alike, not to mention wider society' (Sinclair, 2008, p. 218). Without mediation, the complex nature of the leadership role itself may result in a lack of willingness on the part of educators to take on positional roles. Such complexity intensifies the troubles and challenges for ECEC leadership that have persisted over many years (Gibbs, 2022).

Persistent troubles and challenges for ECEC leadership

Persistent challenges to the enactment of effective leadership within ECEC settings include workforce retention (which results in supply issues for positional leadership roles), a lack of shared understandings of effective leadership, diverse conceptualisations of leadership and undefined pathways to positional leadership roles (Douglass, 2019; Liew, 2017; Muijs et al., 2004). Further, professional learning specifically for leadership is predominantly focused on the development of 'the leader'. Such a focus may cause organisations to overlook the emergence of leadership, the practices of leading by educators and the environments those practices occur within (Lichtenstein et al., 2006; Mistry & Sood, 2012; Zinsser et al., 2016).

Workforce retention and supply issues

There are major concerns about the risks to the workforce and supply issues because of an unstable and poorly educated workforce (Irvine et al., 2016). Irvine et al.'s 2016 study of 1200 degree-qualified ECEC teachers used purposive sampling, case studies and in-depth interviews to research views and attitudes to professional continuity. The researchers found that one in five participants planned to leave their job within a year because of low pay, feeling undervalued and increasing time spent on paperwork. Educators who took up further training or upgraded to an ECEC teaching degree were the most likely to report that they intended to leave the profession. The researchers found that enablers for remaining within the field included personal and professional qualities, opportunities for pedagogical leadership, a sense of professional identity, commitment to play-based teaching and learning, freedom of curriculum, prior long day care experience and long day care business understanding (Irvine et al., 2016). From these findings, it is possible to infer that an enabler for professional continuity and progress could be leadership development that encourages educators in their professional identity, leadership and decision-making autonomy.

The potential benefits of leadership development for the workforce are also cited within international reports and workforce strategies (Australian Children's Quality Authority, 2020; Productivity Commission, 2011). For

Cultivating Leadership in Early Childhood Education and Care

example, in Australia, the Early Years Workforce Strategy (Standing Council on School Education and Early Childhood, 2012) highlights the role that increased qualifications, clearer career pathways and leadership development for educators could play in improving the quality of education and care.

It is essential, however, to emphasise that workforce sustainability challenges cannot be overcome by leadership development and qualification incentivisation alone. Long-term workforce sustainability is a complex matter. The politics of educator practice, inadequate remuneration, the professional status of the work of ECEC and broader social differences, including educational background and employment circumstances of educators, are other contributors to the instability of the workforce (Jackson, 2016). Leadership development should, therefore, be considered within the broader landscape of the ECEC workforce. Additionally, an understanding of leadership effectiveness must underpin any measures for development if leadership is to contribute to the process quality of the ECEC setting (Douglass, 2019; Harrison et al., 2020; Siraj-Blatchford & Manni, 2007).

Lack of shared understanding of 'effective' leadership

Leadership 'effectiveness' remains an under-researched area. Douglass (2019) notes that leadership is 'one of the single most important drivers of organisational performance, quality improvement and innovation' (p. 6), yet only a small number of studies employ rigorous methods measuring the effect of leadership on the quality of ECEC (Douglass, 2019). Divergent theoretical orientations and opposing purposes for ECEC leadership (e.g., compliance versus innovation; see Gibbs et al., 2019; Halttunen et al., 2019; Sims et al., 2014) signal the need to understand what constitutes effective leadership that contributes to the process quality of ECEC programs.

Traditionally, leadership effectiveness, described as 'getting the job done' and 'keeping the group in good working order' (Simons, 1986), was framed as being based on leadership capability, traits and context. In the search for what constitutes leadership 'effectiveness', various tools were developed. Bloom and Sheerer (1992) pioneered the measurement of leadership internationally with marking scales relating to traits and capabilities. Educating and caring for children were central to these measures. By 2003, leadership effectiveness was recognised as an increasingly complex concept. Characteristics of effectiveness were expanded to include competencies, style, self-awareness and authenticity (Bloom, 2003). In 2004, Muijs et al. identified the 'need to identify more precisely what effective ECE leaders do, and, by association, what development is required to maximise the effectiveness of all leaders in ECE' (p. 167). Reaching a consensus on leadership effectiveness has preoccupied professional thinking, opinion and, to a lesser extent, research in recent years (see Fonsén & Soukainen, 2020; Harrison et al., 2020). Researchers have traditionally focused on the styles or behaviours that contribute to effective leadership (Rodd, 2013; Talan & Jorde Bloom, 2004). Moyles (2006) and Sullivan (2010) also produced measurement scales that considered context, behaviour and responsibilities. These scales were piloted in small studies, and their results were inconclusive.

Two key studies in 2007 and 2016 sought to determine the components of effective leadership. The Effective Leadership in Early Years Study (ELEYS) (Siraj-Blatchford & Manni, 2007) investigated leadership in 'effective' ECEC settings. These settings previously participated in the Effective Provision of Preschool Education (EPPE) in the United Kingdom (UK). ELEYS researchers explored the issue of leadership from the 'bottom up' and focused on concrete leadership behaviours rather than leadership beliefs. Semi-structured interviews with centre staff; observations and field notes; desk reviews of manager demographics, centre policies and documentation; and child outcome data were analysed. This study was unique in referencing child outcomes in relation to leadership effectiveness. Siraj-Blatchford and Manni (2007) found that contextual literacy and a commitment to collaboration, critical reflection and children's learning outcomes were fundamental to leadership enactment. The researchers advocated for the enactment of leadership that recognises the multitude of tasks and changing contexts for leaders. This frame could guide the professional development of leaders (Siraj-Blatchford & Manni, 2007).

The second study in 2016 also focused on the 'nature of leadership' effectiveness, this time in 25 high-performing Sure Start centres in the UK (Coleman et al., 2016). Researchers identified the key challenges of leadership (within the literature) and the behaviours and traits used to address these challenges effectively. The research comprised desk reviews, calls for evidence, 25 case studies and 158 interviews with children's centre leaders, local authority staff, senior and frontline staff, and partner agency staff and parents. Three primary challenges were identified: making leadership visible, ensuring positive outcomes for children and dealing with the complexity of change. The study identified behaviours that addressed the challenges and complexities of leading within ECEC settings. The behaviours were identified as follows: having a clear vision to improve outcomes for children and families, engaging responsively with families, using evidence to drive improvements in outcomes, using business skills strategically, facilitating open communication, embracing integrated working, motivating and empowering staff, and being committed to their own learning and development (Coleman et al., 2016). These studies inform descriptors for leadership that are documented in standards within professional and regulatory documents in both Australia (the National Quality Standard in Australia (Australian Children's Education & Care Quality Authority, 2024) and the UK (the Early Years Professional Standards [Department for Education, 2024]).

Richer knowledge about ECEC leadership effectiveness, though developing, is needed. Creating the foundations for studies of effectiveness potentially begins with shared conceptualisations of leadership and an understanding of leadership theory. The conceptualisations and theoretical perspectives of ECEC leadership are, however, diverse.

Diverse conceptualisations of ECEC leadership

Many conceptualisations and definitions of leadership exist in the broad leadership literature. Australian researcher Hills (2012), in her work on sustainable leadership, identified over 132 working definitions of leadership and 40 theories that serve to inform leadership practice. These conceptualisations include models of command and control, transformational, transactional, servant, distributed and collective leadership—also described by Bolman and Deal (2013) and Drucker and Wartzman (2010). ECEC leadership has followed along with these frameworks. As a unique profession, ECEC has not settled on a shared definition of leadership that adequately informs practice or contributes to the development of leadership in ECEC settings (Waniganayake et al., 2023. In 2005, educational theorist Sergiovanni (2005) warned that educational leadership would remain characterless if professions continued to import rather than invent mindscapes and models, concepts and definitions. Researchers maintain that the lack of clarity and the scarcity of research on leadership theory has slowed the development of ECEC leadership over time (Douglass, 2019; Dunlop, 2008; Liew, 2017; Muijs et al., 2004).

Conceptualisations of leadership are considered in greater depth in Chapter 2: "Thinking Differently About Leadership Theory and Practice".

Uncertain pathways to leadership roles

The pathway to positional leadership roles in ECEC is problematic. Many formal leaders assume roles in an 'accidental' rather than 'intentional' way. The phenomenon of accidental leadership is identified in early literature (Schomburg, 1999). Recent research notes that this perception limits the progress of leaders (Heikka et al., 2016; Sims et al., 2014; Vannebo & Gotvassli, 2015). When emerging leaders come to positions unintentionally (e.g., due to a positional leader resigning where no succession planning exists), they may lack the foundational knowledge for the role and feel unprepared to lead.

Several studies have investigated the pathways to positional leadership roles. A study of 351 Australian ECEC leaders (Sims et al., 2014) found that teachers who had unintentionally moved into leadership were not well prepared to perform the role. These leaders held rigid interpretations of leadership and did not value reflection and in-depth discussion for all staff, and this was due to their lack of preparation for the leadership role. The need for leaders to direct, motivate, inspire, model and bring others to new practices was unfulfilled, and educators became disheartened and disempowered under their leadership (Sims et al., 2014).

Hard's 2005 study, a qualitative investigation into understandings of leadership and its enactment among 26 participants in Australian ECEC settings, found that leader performance was shaped and affected by their lack of confidence and ability to articulate the role. The perception of the activity of leadership was influenced by their general knowledge rather than an understanding of leadership within the complex ECEC environment. An important finding was that professional identity and qualifications underpin leaders' agency to lead. The status of the role also had an effect on willingness to take on leadership roles. This suggests that the path to leadership begins at the inception of an educator's career and is influenced by professional growth and perceptions of identity. Aubrey et al. (2013) also noted the difference in leadership enactment according to qualifications; more qualified leaders used rationality, knowledge and reflection as tools for leading, and those less qualified relied on pre-determined strategies and business orientations to drive their leadership.

Likewise, a research project conducted for the Norwegian government on ECEC leadership identity explored the perceptions that leaders held of themselves and their effect on the enactment of the leadership role (Granrusten, 2016). Interviews were conducted with 16 directors of ECEC services, and participants considered how they perceived themselves within both personal and professional identity frames. In the personal frame, directors placed themselves on a continuum from 'uncertain pedagogical professional' to 'certain professional leader'. Choices were influenced by the context of the service (private, public, large, small) and the pathway to leadership. It was found that the perception of the importance of collective professional identity was a foundation for leadership. This research highlights issues of leader preparation, professional identity and the importance of professional routes to leadership that are purposeful and planned.

Research continues to cite the lack of pathways and preparation for teachers to take on leadership roles. For example, Klevering and McNae (2018) and Weisz-Koves (2011) note the loss of potential when teachers are overlooked as prospective leaders. Alchin et al. (2019) urge that an awareness of the development of leaders through the establishment of frameworks encompassing organisational and pedagogical leadership is vital. Researchers note, however, that there is a need for leadership preparation to begin in the undergraduate years and to continue throughout professional service.

Another contribution to the discussion on leadership pathways is a recent study from the UK. The lack of clarity on pathways to leadership is viewed through an alternative lens in this research study by Douglass (2018). The qualitative study of 43 educators reconceptualised leadership as a process of change to ECEC quality and pathways as non-linear. Such a conceptualisation offered the opportunity for educators to co-create pathways within a site's ecosystem. The ecosystem comprised supportive systems and policies, leadership networks and relationships, leadership development programs and supportive workplaces. Douglass noted:

> *Building and co-creating a leadership pathway is exciting, creative, and deeply challenging work. It is time for our field to build the infrastructure to nurture, support, and sustain this work, beyond a handful of individual leadership development programs.*
>
> (Douglass, 2018, p. 395)

The approach to the cultivation of leadership, recommended by Douglass (2018), creates greater opportunity for the emergence and development of leadership within the ECEC setting ecosystem. Other considerations in ECEC leadership professional development are described below and in greater depth in Chapter 6: "Learning for Leading".

Developing ECEC leaders

Professional development for leadership builds sustainable practice and creates future leadership capacity. Professional development has the capacity to ameliorate and disrupt challenges (Gibbs, 2022). Professional development is defined as the transformational process of personal growth and individual experiences that contribute to the development of knowledge and skills and also to the experiences that people engage in to enhance professional skills (Bloom & Rafanello, 1995). Professional development for ECEC leadership receives attention within the literature and research, yet a paucity of empirical research on the development of emerging leaders exists. Waniganayake and Stipanovic (2016) argue that this paucity has led to a lack of structured programs that appropriately focus on building sustainable leadership in ECEC.

Additionally, a long-running debate surrounds the difference between management and leadership. This can lead to confusion about the development of skills and knowledge: what should be developed, how can leadership be developed and what is leadership actually for?

Management

Commonly, 'management' refers to the administrative and operational aspects of running an ECEC service, such as planning, organising, budgeting, staffing and complying with regulations (Fu, 2023). Leadership refers to the vision and direction that guide an ECEC service, such as setting goals, inspiring staff, fostering collaboration and promoting quality improvement. Management appears to rely on technical expertise and rationality, whereas leadership is considered to be visionary and expansive. Is it helpful to consider leadership and management as discrete concepts? Should each be regarded as having exclusive knowledge, skills and values? Rebecca

Cultivating Leadership in Early Childhood Education and Care

describes the unique challenge of both leading and managing people in the ECEC setting:

> But then you've got someone that you also- they need to be almost performance managing. But in the next breath, you're literally working alongside of each other. There's no separation. You're not a leader right then. You can't retire somewhere and go and spend some time gaining your thoughts, you constantly with the people that you're leading, and the leadership parts can be really positive. The visions, the sharing, the goals. But sometimes those management aspects of leadership are very prominent, and you have to manage the people that you're side by side, and I find that personally, really challenging.
>
> –Rebecca, Study 2

Hope and optimism

Despite the challenges, the complex array of tasks and roles and a lack of adequate preparation for ECEC leadership, there is hope for emerging and positional leaders and optimism regarding the potential that high-quality ECEC holds for children's well-being.

Sara describes this hope, optimism and growth:

> I love knowing I am going to preschool where, for the most part, everyone is happy and united in a common goal. We put the children at the centre of all decision making and go from there. I feel as though I am contributing to something larger each day, and that gives me enormous personal satisfaction. I love seeing children progress and grow through the program we provide—more teaching related, but I also feel my leadership enables the learning program to be successful. My colleagues have grown a great deal in a professional capacity with the changes we have introduced in the time I have been the director. It excites me to see them flourish and contribute to the overall success of the preschool. Seeing the program evolve and change over time is so satisfying and validates everything that I love about the ECEC sector.
>
> –Sara, Study 2

Conclusion

The practices of leading and positional leadership are complex and sophisticated activities. Challenges for the enactment of leadership continue, and the leadership narrative must change to ensure a sustainable workforce of leaders in ECEC. Yet the role of leader in its current form is unsustainable. How leadership emerges, develops and is sustained must be reimagined as an organisational responsibility and the opportunity to lead be open to many rather than those in positional roles.

This chapter described those troubles for leadership in depth and lays the groundwork for change to leadership development. In this chapter, you have been introduced to the foundations, challenges, complexities and complications of early childhood leadership. The next chapter explores conceptualisations and theoretical perspectives on leading and leadership, and these conceptualisations will cause you to think differently about leading and leadership.

Reflective questions

Reflect on your own leadership story using the following questions:
Is my pathway into leadership planned or 'accidental'?
How did I think about leadership philosophy and theory before becoming a leader?
How do theory and philosophy inform my practices of leading?
What are my challenges in leading?

References

Alchin, I., Arthur, L. & Woodrow, C. (2019). Evidencing leadership and management challenges in early childhood in Australia. *Australasian Journal of Early Childhood*, *44*(3), 285–297. https://doi.org/10.1177/1836939119855563

Aubrey, C., Godfrey, R. & Harris, A. (2013). How do they manage? An investigation of early childhood leadership. *Educational Management Administration & Leadership*, *41*(1), 5–29. https://doi.org/10.1177/1741143212462702

Australian Children's Education and Care Quality Authority. (2017). Leadership and management in education and care services. An analysis of Quality Area 7 of the National Quality Standard. *Occasional Paper 5*. https://www.acecqa.gov.au/acecqas-occasional-paper-5-quality-area-7

Australian Children's Education and Care Quality Authority. (2024). National Quality Standard https://www.acecqa.gov.au/nqf/national-quality-standard

Australian Children's Education & Care Quality Authority. (2020). *Progressing a national approach to the children's education and care workforce* [Workforce report November 2019]. https://www.acecqa.gov.au/sites/default/files/2020-10/ChildrensEducationandCareNationalWorkforceStrategy_0.pdf

Australian Government Department of Education. (2012). *National quality framework for early childhood education and care* [Archived website]. Archived 6 November 2013, https://web.archive.org/web/20131106141144/https://www.education.gov.au/national-quality-framework-early-childhood-education-and-care

Australian Productivity Commission. (2014). *Childcare and Early Childhood Learning.* https://www.pc.gov.au/inquiries/completed/childcare/report

Bloom, P. J. (2003). *Leadership in action: How effective leaders get things done.* New Horizons.

Bloom, P. J. & Rafanello, D. (1995). The professional development of early childhood center directors: Key elements of effective training models. *Journal of Early Childhood Teacher Education, 16*(1), 3–8. https://doi.org/10.1080/1090102950160102

Bloom, P. J. & Sheerer, M. (1992). The effect of leadership training on child care program quality. *Early Childhood Research Quarterly, 7*(4), 579–594. https://doi.org/10.1016/0885-2006(92)90112-c

Bolman, L. & Deal, T. (2013). *Reframing organizations: Artistry, choice, and leadership* (5th ed.). Wiley.

Brennan, D. (1998). *The politics of Australian child care: Philanthropy to feminism and beyond.* Cambridge University Press.

Coleman, A., Sharp, C. & Handscomb, G. (2016). Leading highly performing children's centres: Supporting development of the 'accidental leaders'. *Educational Management Administration & Leadership, 44*(5), 775–793. https://doi.org/10.1177/1741143215574506

Department for Education. (2024). *Early years qualification requirements and standards.* Department for Education United Kingdom.

Douglass, A. (2018). Redefining leadership: Lessons from an early education leadership development initiative. *Early Childhood Education Journal, 46*(4), 387–396. https://doi.org/10.1007/s10643-017-0871-9

Douglass, A. (2019). Leadership for quality early childhood education and care. *OECD Education Working Paper* (No. 211). OECD Publishing. https://doi.org/10.1787/6e563bae-en

Drucker, P. & Wartzman, R. (2010). *The Drucker lectures: Essential lessons on management, society, and economy.* McGraw Hill.

Dunlop, A. (2008). *A Literature Review on Leadership in the Early Years.* Scottish Government. https://www.academia.edu/30192102/A_Literature_Review_on_Leadership_in_the_Early_Years?auto=download

Fonsén, E. & Soukainen, U. (2020). Sustainable pedagogical leadership in Finnish early childhood education (ECE): An evaluation by ECE professionals. *Early Childhood Education Journal, 48*(2), 213–222. https://doi.org/10.1007/s10643-019-00984-y

Fu, W. (2023). A critical examination of effective leadership in early childhood education. *Journal of Educational Leadership and Policy Studies, 7*(1), article 16. https://go.southernct.edu/jelps/

Gibbs, L. (2022). Leadership emergence and development: Organizations shaping leading in early childhood education. *Educational Management Administration & Leadership, 50*(4), 672–693. https://doi.org/10.1177/1741143220940324

Gibbs, L., Press, F. & Wong, S. (2019). Compliance in a landscape of complexity: Regulation and educational leadership. In L. Gibbs & M. Gasper (Eds.), *Challenging the intersection of policy with pedagogy* (pp. 159–174). Routledge.

Granrusten, P. (2016). Early Childhood Teacher or Leader? Early Childhood Directors' Perceptions of Their Identity. *Journal of Early Childhood Research, 5*(2), 247–267.

Halttunen, L., Sims, M., Waniganayake, M., Hadley, F., Bøe, M., Hognestad, K. & Heikka, J. (2019). Working as early childhood centre directors and deputies: Perspectives from Australia, Finland and Norway. In P. Strehmel, J. Heikka, E. Hujala, J Rodd & M. Waniganayake (Eds.), *Leadership in early education in times of change: Research from five continents* (pp. 231–252). Verlag Barbara Budrich.

Harrison, L., Hadley, H., Irvine, I., Davis, B., Barblett, L., Hatzigianni, M. & Li, R. (2020). *Quality improvement research project.* Macquarie University and the Australian Children's Education & Care Quality Authority. https://www.acecqa.gov.au/resources/research#QIR, https://www.acecqa.gov.au/sites/default/files/2020-05/quality-improvement-research-project-2019.PDF

Heckman, J. (2011). The economics of inequality: The value of early childhood education. *American Educator, 35*(1), 31–47. https://www.aft.org/ae/spring2011/heckman

Heikka, J., Halttunen, L., & Waniganayake, M. (2016). Perceptions of early childhood education professionals on teacher leadership in Finland. *Early Child Development and Care,* 1–14. https://doi.org/10.1080/03004430.2016.1207066

Hills, L. (2012). *Lasting female educational leadership: Leadership legacies of women leaders* (Vol. 18). Springer Science & Business Media.

Irvine, S. L., Thorpe, K. J., McDonald, P., Lunn, J. & Sumsion, J. (2016). *Money, love and identity: Initial findings from the National ECEC Workforce study* [Summary report from the national ECEC Workforce Development Policy Workshop, Brisbane, Queensland]. Queensland University of Technology. https://eprints.qut.edu.au/101622/1/Brief_report_ECEC_Workforce_Development_Policy_Workshop_final.pdf

Jackson, J. (2016). The view from the helicopter: Examining the Australian early childhood workforce using the national census of population and housing. *Australasian Journal of Early Childhood, 41*(4), 72–79. https://doi.org/10.1177/183693911604100409

Kamerman, S. B. & Gatenio-Gabel, S. (2007). Early childhood education and care in the United States: An overview of the current policy picture. *International Journal of Child Care and Education Policy (Seoul), 1*(1), 23–34. https://doi.org/10.1007/2288-6729-1-1-23

Klevering, N. & McNae, R. (2018). Making sense of leadership in early childhood education: Tensions and complexities between concepts and practices. *Journal of Educational Leadership, Policy and Practice, 33*(1), 5–17. https://doi.org/10.21307/jelpp-2018-002

Lichtenstein, B., Uhl-Bien, M., Marion, R., Seers, A., Orton, J. D. & Schreiber, C. (2006). Complexity leadership theory: An interactive perspective on leading in complex adaptive systems. *Emergence: Complexity and Organization, 8*(4), 2–12. https://digitalcommons.unl.edu/managementfacpub/8

Liew, J. (2017). *A systematic review on strategies for leadership development in the early childhood sector–applicability to the Singapore context.* Evidence for Policy and Practice Information and Co-ordinating Centre (EPPI-Centre) Social Science Research Unit. https://eppi.ioe.ac.uk/cms/Default.aspx?tabid=3746

Mistry, M. & Sood, K. (2012). Challenges of Early Years leadership preparation: a comparison between early and experienced Early Years practitioners in England. *Management in Education, 26*(1), 28–37. https://doi.org/10.1177/0892020611427068

Moyles, J. (2006). *Effective leadership and management in the early years.* Open University Press.

Muijs, D., Aubrey, C., Harris, A. & Briggs, A. (2004). How do they manage?: A review of the research on leadership in early childhood. *Journal of Early Childhood Research, 2*(2), 157–169. https://doi.org/10.1177/1476718X04042974

Organisation for Economic Co-operation and Development. (2020). *Building a high-quality early childhood education and care workforce: Further results from the starting strong survey 2018.* OECD Publishing. https://doi.org/10.1787/b90bba3d-en

Press, F. & Hayes, A. (2000). *OECD thematic review of early childhood education and care policy.* Commonwealth Government of Australia. https://www.oecd.org/australia/1900259.pdf

Productivity Commission. (2011). *Early childhood development workforce* [Productivity Commission research report]. https://www.pc.gov.au/inquiries/completed/education-workforce-early-childhood/report/early-childhood-report.pdf

Rodd, J. (2013). *Leadership in early childhood: the pathway to professionalism* (4th ed.). Allen & Unwin.

Rothfuss, P. (2010). *The name of the wind: The kingkiller chronicle: Book 1.* Hachette.

Schomburg, R. L. (1999). Leadership development in early childhood education. *Journal of Early Childhood Teacher Education, 20*(2), 215–219. https://doi.org/10.1080/0163638990200224

Sergiovanni, T. (2005). *Leadership: What's in it for Schools?* (Vol. 36243). Routledge.

Simons, J. (1986). *Administering early childhood services.* Sydney College of Advanced Education.

Sims, M., Forrest, R., Semann, A. & Slattery, C. (2014). Conceptions of early childhood leadership: Driving new professionalism? *International Journal of Leadership in Education, 18*(2), 149–166. https://doi.org/10.1080/13603124.2014.962101

Sinclair, A. (2008). *Leadership for the disillusioned: Moving beyond myths and heroes to leading that liberates*. Allen & Unwin.

Siraj-Blatchford, I. & Manni, L. (2007). *Effective leadership in the early years sector: The ELEYS study*. Institute of Education, University of London.

Standing Council on School Education and Early Childhood. (2012). *Early years workforce strategy*. Australian Government Department of Education, Skills and Employment. Website archived 21 March 2015, https://web.archive.org/web/20150321105634/https://docs.education.gov.au/node/2918

Sullivan, D. (2010). *Learning to lead*. Red Leaf Press.

Sylva, K. (2010). *Early childhood matters: Evidence from the effective pre-school and primary education project*. Taylor & Francis.

Talan, T., & Jorde Bloom, P. (2004). *Program administration scale: measuring early childhood leadership and management*. Teachers College Press.

Torii, K., Fox, S., & Cloney, D. (2017). *Quality is key in early childhood education in Australia*. www.mitchellinstitute.org.au

Vannebo, B., & Gotvassli, K. (2015). The concept of strategy in the early childhood education and care sector. *European Early Childhood Education Research Journal*, 1–15. https://doi.org/10.1080/1350293X.2015.1102410

Waniganayake, M. & Stipanovic, S. (2016). Advancing leadership capacity: Preparation of early childhood leaders in Australia through a coursework Masters degree. *Journal of Early Childhood Education Research*, 5(2, Special Issue), 268–288. https://journal.fi/jecer/article/view/114061

Waniganayake, M., Cheeseman, S., Fenech, M., Hadley, F., & Shepherd, W. (2023). *Leadership: contexts and complexities in early childhood education* (3rd ed.). Oxford University Press

Weisz-Koves, T. (2011). Developing teacher leadership in early childhood education in Aotearoa through a potential-based approach. *Journal of Educational Leadership, Policy and Practice*, 26(2), 35–47. https://search.informit.org/doi/10.3316/informit.805275046795112

Zinsser, K. M., Denham, S. A., Curby, T. W. & Chazan-Cohen, R. (2016). Early childhood directors as socializers of emotional climate. *Learning Environments Research*, 19(2), 267–290. https://doi.org/10.1007/s10984-016-9208-7

Thinking Differently About Leadership Theory and Practice

This chapter

- explores theories and conceptualisations of leadership in early childhood education and care
- introduces perspectives on leading and leadership
- presents theory and practice on leading and leadership
- tells stories of theory in current practice and presents philosophies of leadership.

Introduction

This book seeks to disrupt the current narrative on the positional leader's role and the way leadership emerges and develops. The way leadership is conceptualised in early childhood education and care (ECEC) determines this path of development and the shaping of the positional leadership role and gives an understanding of the practice traditions of leadership in ECEC. According to Kemmis et al. (2014), the unfolding practice is shaped by the ways of thinking, doing and relating, influenced by the traditions of the site. Therefore, in this chapter, conceptualisations of leadership theory and practice are explored. These theories and conceptualisations are situated in the contemporary context and build on the work of scholars such as Rodd (2013), Stamopoulos and Barblett (2018) and Waniganayake et al. (2023). Theoretical accounts include traditional leadership theory, distributed leadership, complexity leadership theory (CLT), complex adaptive systems (CAS) and practice theories.

A story of conceptualising and shaping leadership

I have a leadership role and have completed a lot of leadership training and reading, so what is my leadership philosophy?

I am an introvert; I love planning and organising but prefer not to be in the person up the front in the spotlight. I get satisfaction seeing my plans come to fruition and revel in being able to do things my way. So why have I chosen this role, this all-consuming, never-ending, responsible role?

What shapes the leader I am today? I see myself as an enabling leader, one who sees the big picture, trusts those around me and wants to see them develop and grow. Why is this? What shapes me comes from past experiences and knowledge. Before I gained the knowledge, I took on a lot from my past experiences, really taking on board how I was treated and how I would like to treat others.

In my first year as an ECEC leader, I was fortunate to participate in a leadership program. This year-long program helped me really look at myself as a leader for the first time. It provided structure to learn ways of managing myself and cementing what I wanted for my team. This was the first time that I was exposed to leadership and sociology theorists such as Jim Collins, researchers like Brene Brown and Simon Sinek. I was engaged and enthralled learning about myself and sharing this with my team.

The learning I did led me to understand that building people's capacity to understand themselves meant they would also be able to understand those around them and create deeper relationships with these people. People who are invested in one another support one another and work better together.

–Shannon, Study 1

Conceptualisations of ECEC leadership: Looking back

The literature on leadership points to vast and varied conceptualisations and definitions. As highlighted in Chapter 1, a plethora of working definitions and theories inform leadership practice (Hills, 2012). The theories ranging from command and control to transformational, transactional, servant,

Cultivating Leadership in Early Childhood Education and Care

distributed and collective leadership are discussed in Bolman and Deal (2013) and Drucker and Wartzman (2010).

Although ECEC leadership has adopted these theoretical frameworks, there remains the lack of agreed definition and conceptualisation for ECEC persists. This is a problem for the emergence and cultivation of leadership and leading as the filed grapples with how to foster and practice leadership (Waniganayake et al., 2023). It is therefore essential that a distinct identity and conceptualisation is carved out as this would allow the field to realise its full potential (Brownlee et al., 2010).

A number of studies on theoretical models for leadership within the ECEC environment are evident in the international arena. These studies individually differ in their theorising on leadership models. Some reference the development of a highly structured ECEC leadership model (e.g., Aubrey et al., 2013; Li, 2015), while other scholars call for a rethink of leadership conceptualisations to account for feminist and traditional ECEC origins (e.g., Bøe & Hognestad, 2015; Davis et al., 2015; Gibbs et al., 2019; Mettiäinen, 2016).

Researchers maintain that a lack of clarity and the scarcity of research on leadership theory have slowed the development of ECEC leadership over time (Douglass, 2019; Dunlop, 2008; Liew, 2017; Muijs et al., 2004), but more recently an increased focus and volume of research signals a change.

A theoretical timeline of ECEC leadership

Command and control leadership: Theoretical conceptualisations of leadership in ECEC, originally adopted from masculine business models, seem at odds with the purpose and feminist history of ECEC leadership (Davis et al., 2015). In 2004, Muijs et al. highlighted the need to empirically test leadership models within ECEC settings and posited that components of the leadership activity were focused more on 'maintenance' (management) than development (leadership). They asserted that leadership in ECEC had transitioned from its traditions as a gendered, feminist activity to a masculinised endeavour. The conventional masculine leadership style is characterised by task orientation, delegation and charismatic and sovereign leadership, whereas the feminine leadership style is characterised by a desire to progress and transform people and organisations (Davis et al., 2015; Muijs et al., 2004). International leadership scholars in ECEC acknowledge that traditional leadership theory is not well aligned with contemporary ECEC practice (Rodd, 2013; Waniganayake et al., 2023) and have variously sought

36

to identify a conceptual frame of management, administration and leadership that accommodates the shifting conditions where ECEC leadership is enacted (Gibbs et al., 2019).

Command and control leadership is sometimes enacted as 'micro-management' of people and tasks within ECEC settings and organisations. Fisher et al. (2021) note that autonomy is more conducive to people's improved performance than oversight and that people have strong emotional and psychological reactions to unnecessary and unwanted help. Complex, cognitively demanding work requires leaders to engage deeply:

> *I felt the overwhelming responsibility of having to know everything. I was the one with the training, and I was being paid as the director of the centre. If I didn't know what to do, I thought I had let the team down, and everyone would see that I was terrified. I kept my eyes on everything and everyone—always providing a solution and answers to funding challenges, programming, health, safety … it was exhausting.*
> *—Laney, Study 2*

Support is ideally delivered in a timely manner and without overt control (which diminishes dignity and autonomy). In a study of leaders over ten years in the United States (US), Fisher et al. (2021) found that pre-empting problems and stepping in to assist early could be perceived as micro-management. A more successful strategy is to be available and ready to respond:

> *The team was so patient. They realised I was young and let me have enough space to grow into my leadership. Eventually, I realised I had this gold mine of knowledge in the team. For example, our nurse would deal with all of the health issues and parents respected her knowledge. If she said a child wasn't well, the parents would be in to pick them up immediately. Our cook, who was a nutritionist, was the go-to on all matters related to diet and food. Our admin was a whizz at funding matters and could find money everywhere. In lots of ways, I just needed to be the cheer squad, not the task master. What a relief!*
> *—Laney, Study 2*

Cultivating Leadership in Early Childhood Education and Care

'Great Man' and trait theory: The Great Man theory in leadership is a historical perspective that suggests that extraordinary individuals possess inherent traits and qualities that make them natural leaders. The Great Man theory emerged during the 19th century and gained prominence in leadership studies, primarily in the 20th century (Drucker & Wartzman, 2010). This theory posits that leadership is an intrinsic characteristic and that great leaders are born, not made. While historically influential, the Great Man theory has received criticism for several reasons. First, it implies that leadership is open to only a few individuals and additionally that leadership for less confident people seems unachievable.

Trait theory, conversely, is a contemporary approach that explores the idea of leadership traits and characteristics; although it departs from the notion of 'Great Men', trait theory suggests that leaders still possess special attributes, such as intelligence, confidence, charisma and determination, that contribute to their leadership effectiveness. While trait theory acknowledges that some people may naturally possess these traits, it does not limit leadership to a select few. Instead, it emphasises leadership potential in a broader range of individuals (Drucker & Wartzman, 2010).

Trait theory has evolved to incorporate the understanding that leadership traits can be developed, refined and leveraged in various contexts. This perspective aligns with the belief that leadership is a dynamic and adaptable quality that can be cultivated and harnessed by a broader group of individuals. Trait theory emphasises that leadership is not limited to a select few but can be cultivated and developed in people who possess or are willing to develop the necessary traits and characteristics.

Tucker (2019), in an investigation on traits and characteristics of 12 ECEC leaders in high-quality services in four countries, asked: what are the self-reported characteristics and personality traits of successful leaders in high-quality early childhood programs? Leaders responded heterogeneously, but they commonly focused on ethics, honesty and persistence. They also described themselves as self-confident, positive and empowering. These research findings are interesting and lead to questions about knowledge, skills and values. For example, were the ECEC leaders reflecting on disposition or perhaps personal values? The disposition of leaders is a topic taken up in Chapter 3.

Transformational leadership: According to Jung (2004), transformational leadership 'emphasises leadership practices that motivate followers to aspire to the common good of society rather than self-interest' (p. 1). In early

38

Thinking Differently About Leadership Theory and Practice

childhood settings, transformational leadership may be enacted for the good of children, families, educators or organisational objectives. For example, transformational leaders create visions and environments to inspire educators. People often feel they can excel beyond their expectations when they are in the presence of a transformational leader (Stewart, 2006).

According to Brownlee et al. (2010), transformational leaders have four main characteristics that influence their staff positively. First, they foster trust and respect among their staff by being ideal role models. Second, they inspire their staff to be more engaged and committed to the organisation's vision and goals. Third, they stimulate their staff's creativity and learning by challenging them to think in new and innovative ways. Fourth, they interact with their staff individually and tailor their support and feedback according to each staff member's needs and performance. These characteristics help transformational leaders to promote 'appropriate workplace behaviour' among their staff (Sarros & Santora, 2001, p. 385). Transformational leadership will, therefore, engender innovation and originality and provide guidance for and earn the commitment of their staff.

Educators often speak about leaders as transformational:

> *My director is there for me. She makes everything possible—I want to work hard for her and be that person she looks to, to make the babies room work.*
>
> —Callo, Study 1

However, it is clear that more than mere individual enactment of leadership is taking place; it is more than inspiration and encouragement. Providing guidance and material resources and having expectations of team behaviour are also essential aspects of the transformational leader:

> *But making that work is only possible because she sets clear boundaries and provides me with the resources I need. There are some matters of practice that are non-negotiable ... working as a team, meeting our job responsibilities and being clear with each other about expectations.*
>
> —Callo, Study 1

Cultivating Leadership in Early Childhood Education and Care

***Distributed leadership*:** Distributed leadership originated as a response to the limitations of traditional, top-down leadership models. It gained prominence in educational contexts during the late 20th century. Distributed leadership challenges the notion that leadership is the exclusive domain of a single individual; instead, it suggests that leadership can and should be shared among the individuals of an organisation (Waniganayake et al., 2023).

Distributed leadership, often referred to as shared leadership or collective leadership, envisions a leadership structure in which various individuals at different levels of an organisation contribute to the overall leadership function. What distributed leadership looks like can vary depending on the specific context and organisation, but some key features are consistent.

According to Spillane (2012), distributed leadership offers six main benefits for organisations. (1) Distributed leadership encourages collaboration among individuals with diverse skills and perspectives, influencing the organisation's direction. (2) In this theory, leadership responsibilities are shared across multiple leaders rather than centralised in one individual. (3) This approach is adaptable to change, allowing leaders to emerge based on their expertise and situational context. (4) Distributed leadership empowers team members at all levels to lead within their areas of knowledge, boosting their engagement and sense of ownership. (5) Additionally, it nurtures a culture of learning, welcoming new ideas, feedback and innovation. (6) Lastly, it establishes collective accountability for the organisation's success, promoting teamwork to achieve common objectives (Spillane, 2012).

Overall, distributed leadership reflects a democratic and inclusive approach. This form of leadership promotes a more adaptive and responsive leadership structure that can better navigate the complexities and challenges of today's rapidly changing environments. Yet distributed leadership is troubled in the ECEC profession.

For example, Aubrey et al. (2013) investigated leadership theory and modelling in a study of 194 formal and informal leaders within a diverse range of ECEC settings in the UK. While participants in this study preferred a collaborative, distributed model, the model was situated in a hierarchical organisational structure. The authors identified the implementation of a contingent, contextual leadership model and suggested that there was a lack of understanding of leadership theory by the leaders themselves. Participants

Thinking Differently About Leadership Theory and Practice

were conflicted about performing leadership in a culture that was counter to their own beliefs.

A cross-cultural study of 100 principals of ECEC sites was conducted in Finland, Japan and Singapore by Hujala et al. (2016). They found that participants preferred a model of distributed leadership; however, this model was not fully enacted, as pedagogical leadership did not genuinely involve the ECEC teachers. The research by Hujala et al. (2016) echoed the findings of research on distributed leadership in ECEC by Heikka et al. (2013). Heikka et al. (2013) noted that without an acknowledgement of the interdependencies of leadership enactments between actors, a distributed model was rarely used. Further, recent examination of distributed leadership highlights the paradox of a form of leading that is dependent upon a hierarchical structure where accountability and compliance ensure the meeting of standards and the hoarding of knowledge (Raelin, 2018). In this context, we see 'hierarchical conditions largely persisting and when democratic leadership occurs it only does so with the permission of those in control' (Raelin, 2018, p. 621).

Heikka et al. (2013) also found that distributed leadership is a contextual and relational phenomenon that depends on the interactions and interdependencies of multiple stakeholders, such as teachers, centre directors and municipal leaders. Findings of Heikka et al. and Waniganayake et al. show that distributed leadership

- can enhance the quality of ECEC by promoting collaborative decision-making, shared responsibility, flexibility, empowerment, continuous learning and collective accountability
- requires a supportive organisational culture, clear role expectations, effective communication and professional development opportunities for all leaders
- is not a fixed or static model but a dynamic and evolving process that can be influenced by various factors, such as policy changes, leadership transitions and external pressures (Heikka et al., 2013).

Generative leadership: Generative leadership is a transformative approach that aims to leave the world in a better state than it was found (Wilson et al., 2020). Generative leadership and early childhood leadership share fundamental principles that shape their strategies. For example, generative and early childhood leaders recognise the importance of a holistic view and the broader effect of their decisions beyond immediate outcomes. Generative leaders encourage creativity and innovation, reimagine possibilities and adapt to changing circumstances. Adaptability and flexibility are characteristic of generative leadership; these qualities or practices are essential within ECEC. Generative leaders focus on relationships and trust. Collaboration and empowerment are central to this type of leadership, which is also significant in ECEC leadership. Creating long-term effects is also a hallmark of generative leaders.

Collective leadership: Collective leadership is an appealing concept for ECEC researchers, as the characteristics of collective leadership are confluent with the complexity of ECEC settings. These include leadership decentralisation, relationships and influence and patterns of leadership. Collective leadership is also an advance on familiar themes of distributed and contextual leadership where a defined leader or set of leaders utilises skills in a dynamic environment for an identified outcome.

A study by Norwegian researchers Bøe and Hognestad (2015) identified the use of collective theories of leadership in ECEC settings. They analysed teacher leadership as a collaborative, interdependent activity and introduced a hybrid model of collaborative-distributed leadership. This innovative research project used a qualitative shadowing methodology with ECEC teacher leaders. The researchers investigated what characterised teacher leadership with the use of two 'shadows', one conducting interviews and the other taking video observations. A unique teacher leadership was revealed with the teacher both influencing the performance of educators and addressing situational factors that affected the smooth operation of the setting. The hybrid form of collaborative-distributed leadership promoted equality within the setting (Bøe & Hognestad, 2015).

Complexity leadership theory: A reconceptualisation of ECEC leadership through a CLT lens is explored in the Australian context by Gibbs et al. (2019). CLT is derived from complexity theory (Uhl-Bien & Arena, 2017) and can be used to make sense of leadership within the ECEC setting. The theory is concerned with emergence and self-organisation in complex environments (Uhl-Bien & Arena, 2017; Wilkinson & Kemmis, 2014). Further, in this theory, leadership encompasses leading and management. Such a theory integrates key elements of the ECEC positional leader's role, which resists binary conceptualisations of leadership and management (Marion, 2008; Marion & Gonzales, 2013).

Complexity leadership and its application in ECEC

Together, CLT and CAS theory challenge conventional perspectives that measure effectiveness solely by predictable outcomes and the maintenance of equilibrium. Instead, these theories demand a paradigm shift that recognises the inherent surprises and the flexibility within complex environments (Uhl-Bien & Marion, 2007).

CLT emphasises patterns over individual leaders. Rather than fixating on specific leaders, it directs attention to recognisable patterns within organisations. Formal leadership takes a secondary role, while broader organising effects—encompassing both individual practices and complex system dynamics—take precedence (Gibbs, 2022). As a result, the complexity itself generates creativity, which leads to innovative solutions and the establishment of new structures essential for contemporary organisations. CLT resides within CAS, which are dynamic cultures characterised by disequilibrium and unexpected outcomes (Gibbs et al., 2019). In CAS, unexpected outcomes and adaptive responses are embraced. Applying complexity theory to ECEC addresses critical aspects of leading and leadership.

CLT recognises ECEC's complexity. Settings and organisations are intricate, multifaceted environments, and the theory acknowledges this complexity by emphasising the importance of emerging leadership. Complexity theory also recognises the need for adaptive leadership in ECEC contexts.

The use of CLT additionally provides a framework and guidance for emerging leaders; thus, they avoid the 'accidental' leader pathway. Complexity leadership challenges traditional norms, encourages adaptability and critical reflection and recognises that effective leadership emerges collectively from the intricate dynamics of complex systems. Its application in ECEC aligns with the dynamic nature of ECEC practice (Gibbs et al., 2019).

CLT was found to be a valuable lens for Australian ECEC leaders during times of crisis. In Study 2, an analysis of leaders' data through the CLT lens (see Figure 2.1) enabled a unique perspective on the practices of leading in critical periods such as the Pandemic. Figure 2.1 highlights the practices of leadership, through a complexity leadership lens, that were enacted to ensure the well-being and ongoing operation of ECEC during times of crisis. The positional and emerging leaders noted that innovation and creativity were important during these times, and this innovation and creativity had different meanings for each person.

Cultivating Leadership in Early Childhood Education and Care

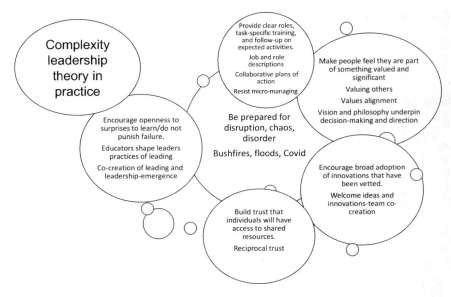

Figure 2.1 An analysis of leaders' data through the CLT lens.

In conversation: What do innovation and creativity look like to you?

In Study 2, leaders were asked: what do innovation and creativity—characteristics of CLT—look like to you? The following are examples of their answers:

> *Using your strengths, being brave and looking outside your comfort zone. Ensuring that your leadership allows each person to use their strengths and feel brave enough to try something new, a culture of no mistakes just learning opportunities.*
> —Kim, Study 2

> *Creativity and innovation mean different things at different times. Both words evoke images of being able to act freely and to be able to bring about effective change as needed. It means having the time, funds, leeway, trust and thinking to get in with each day and to be able to implement exciting and new ways of thinking, being and doing.*
> —Sara, Study 2

Thinking Differently About Leadership Theory and Practice

> *Using you strengths, being brave and looking outside you comfort zone. Ensuring that your leadership allows each person to use their strengths and feel brave enough to try something new, a culture of no mistakes just learning opportunities.*
>
> —Rhonda, Study 2

> *Being able to make changes, work out challenges, be excited about new ideas/concepts, looking towards others with experience/skills to plan/design/contribute to new aspects of the environment/program. Being excited by change.*
>
> —Naomi, Study 2

Practice theory and its application to leading and leadership

Leadership-as-practice

Defined by a fundamental belief that leadership occurs as practice rather than as a replicable set of traits and characteristics (Raelin, 2016), 'leadership-as-practice' increases the opportunity for all educators to be involved in the experience of leading. Further, leading can be conceptualised as a socially just practice occurring as a relational activity with collective approaches. It is a dynamic activity that can be undertaken by anyone and is not limited to those in formal leadership roles. Leading is practised for the shared responsibility of the educational development of children and teachers rather than to achieve organisational goals, although this can be an outcome (Wilkinson, 2017; Wilkinson et al., 2010). In this framing, leading is considered a practice or set of practices.

This framing flips the leadership story. Leadership theory commonly focuses on the organisational outcomes of the leadership effort as highlighted in Chapter 1. Leading as a practice is an energetic, vibrant activity driven by ethics and social justice. Leading, in this context, embodies a complex, diverse and rich set of practices in an equally complex, diverse and rich landscape (Gibbs, 2022).

In addition to these reflections and the theoretical framing of the array of local and international perspectives on leadership, there is agreement that it

Cultivating Leadership in Early Childhood Education and Care

is no longer appropriate to invest power only in positional leaders to achieve an organisation's mission (see Douglass, 2018; Sinclair, 2008; Waniganayake et al., 2023). Contemporary leadership theory moves beyond individualised and centralised approaches.

O'Neill and Brinkerhoff (2018) argue that the capacity to bring about change, execute high-quality pedagogy and smoothly operate ECEC settings is now dependent on collective action and interdependent relationships within ECEC settings.

Contractor et al. (2012) note that a great deal of broad leadership research in recent years has focused on emergent, collectively enacted practices. This is a dynamic approach to shared leadership that shifts from 'understanding the actions and interactions of "leaders" to understanding the emergent, informal and dynamic "leadership" brought about by the members of the collective itself' (p. 995).

Contemporary conceptualisations are moving away from an individualised, charismatic form of leadership to a shared collective approach enacted through the practices of leadership. At this stage, however, international research shows that the profession is still unprepared to engage in wholly democratised collective leadership that is open to those in both formal and informal roles (Klevering & McNae, 2018). If collective leadership is a potential model for ECEC leadership, it is, therefore, important to understand how collectivity is developed and supported, how relationships are created for high-quality ECEC education and the underlying feature of leadership pathways.

Using theory to conceptualise your own leadership philosophy

Theory is an essential component of developing a personal philosophy of leadership. Although theory is conceptually and pragmatically challenging, a theoretical orientation is helpful in positioning and generating a philosophy. According to Nicolini (2012), by using theory it is possible to over-intellectualise common social phenomena (such as leadership), but theory should not be overlooked in practice.

Leadership theories can, therefore, help shape and refine a personal leadership philosophy by providing clarity and intentionality and a framework for reflection. Theory also helps educators understand their own values as a foundation for decision-making in leadership. Trust is also established when a personal leadership philosophy is shared. Further, greater self-awareness and growth are engendered through the important thinking and practice of

46

developing a personal leadership philosophy. Gibbs (2024) found that, despite the clarity of developing a theoretically informed philosophy, less than fifty per cent of positional leaders used theory in their positioning and philosophy on leadership. When the importance of theory was discussed, however, many agreed they would integrate theory and practice in their leadership in the future.

Developing a leadership philosophy regardless of position

It is important to remember that leadership is not open solely to positional leaders. Regardless of your position, you can develop your leadership philosophy. A group of Australian undergraduate early childhood teachers who work in the field and are formal and informal leaders developed their philosophies as an exercise in their leadership studies (personal communication, March, 2024). Undergraduate students' theoretically informed leadership philosophies demonstrate the capacity that critical reflection has in shaping leadership philosophies and the leaders of the future. As you read the following philosophies, reflect on the leadership theories and conceptualisations that have informed their development. Theories, conceptualisations and practices are also highlighted in bold to bring attention to important elements of the philosophies.

Theoretically informed leadership philosophies: Undergraduate perspectives

> Within my current role, I am continuously working on being a **transformational leader**. I believe that it is important to create an environment where educators feel they are able to approach me with their concerns as I work hard to create **open and honest communication** with the educators that I work with. I strive to be a leader that has drive to change but will endeavour to gain all stakeholders views so a decision can be made collaboratively.
>
> –Kim

> As a **transformational leader**, I strive to **inspire and motivate** those around me while also implementing **distributed leadership theory** (Stamopoulos & Barblett, 2018). My approach to leadership and management is centered around **encouraging quality practice and providing feedback** to my team.
>
> –Abby

I believe the most important aspects of being a leader is being **respectful, honest, responsive, being an effective communicator**, a great listener and a supportive leader who gives positive feedback to colleagues. It is also important to be a great team player who involves everyone in the decision making process and respects these views accordingly. I strongly believe it is important to build confidence for colleagues, **involve everyone in pedagogical practices and curriculum processes**. It is also important to give opportunities for staff professional development sessions **to build open positive communication and confidence**. Moreover, as a leader it is important to guide, mentor and nurture staff to the best of your ability to allow staff to become experienced educators.

–Grace

Distributed leadership is a leadership style that I have been working towards. I firmly believe that a correct set of values and professional ethics serve as the benchmark for regulating the behaviour of team members and constitute the cornerstone for guiding children to develop a proper worldview and set of values.

–Hashi

On a professional level, I contend that early childhood education leaders must **continually enhance their personal expertise and teaching skills**, *which not only involves setting clear educational objectives but also requires meticulous design of instructional content and learning activities based on the needs and interests of children, ensuring the coherence of the teaching process, and providing students with profound learning experiences.*

–Jo

Moreover, I think that **effective communication and collaboration skills** *are equally crucial qualities that ECEC leaders should prioritise. By maintaining an* **open mindset, listening, and understanding the needs and opinions of team members, children, and their families**, *we can efficiently convey information and address issues, better meeting the expectations of all stakeholders.*

–Tina

Thinking Differently About Leadership Theory and Practice

My leadership philosophy is to **create an integrated environment** *where everyone with a diverse background, ability, culture, language, skills, value, passions, and uniqueness have an* **equal opportunity to contribute and collaborate with one another** *to create a diverse community that grows in harmony and commits to achieve the best outcomes for the children.*

–Ervina

I firmly believe in **strength-based leadership,** *which recognises and respects the value of all staff members. Every individual has unique strengths, and* **a good leader acknowledges and utilizes them effectively.** *When educators feel confident about their own skills, they can inspire confidence in the children they teach.*

–Monika

I believe **in transformational leadership** *as I implement my leadership responsibilities based on ethical practices that inspire, motivate, recognise individual strengths, and* **create a positive and respectful environment** *where educators can express their views and ideas to meet team goals. I see myself as a visionary leader who demonstrates the capacity to think clearly and strategically. I believe in* **distributed leadership,** *as successful leadership depends on the team members' contribution and involvement. I see the goals being reached more efficiently if tasks are delegated to people whose skills fit the undertaking.*

–Faith

My **leadership philosophy is based on working together towards a shared goal** *while maintaining personal growth and development as an educator. I want to empower my team to be the best they can be in their teaching journeys alongside children, families, and the community in an ever changing environment that is ECE [early childhood education]! I know from experience—and our readings and zoom meetings—that* **context plays a vital role in what kind of leader you can be,** *and I am very lucky to be in a service that has the same outlook as I do, and that is to move the ECE field forward as a professional and integral part of our society, and change the thinking that often saddles us with the 'nice ladies' and 'baby sitting' stigmas to one that gives our profession—and those who work within it—the respect* *and support we deserve. After all, we are creating and laying down the foundations for the children who are our worlds tomorrow! That's kind of a big deal!*

–Jade

*I believe leadership in the early years is a **continual personal and professional process of growth and learning**. It requires the knowledge and skills to use strength-based communication in an ever-changing environment, amongst various contexts and with a diverse range of people from many backgrounds. It is in this communication with others that critical thinking can occur, and change can be made.*

–Sophie

*Leadership plays a significant role to spark inspiration in others and develop a foundation for team building and professional learning. By using **strength-based communication**, leaders can positively impact and guide others to see their strengths and successes, which then flows through the thoughts and actions of others.*

–Grace

*I would like to be a leader who demonstrates **innovation, commitment to personal growth and the growth of others, positivity, and effective collaboration**. I believe leadership is being responsive, listening and taking on board the ideas of others while supporting the team in their individual professional growth. I believe listening and taking on board the ideas of others is a foundation for **distributed leadership theory**, where everyone can contribute and where new leaders realise their strengths and ability to contribute.*

–Jessica

*My leadership philosophy is grounded in **positivity, role modelling, and passion**. I believe in leading by example, embodying **enthusiasm and dedication** in everything I do, **inspiring others** to follow suit. I guide my team to ensure our practices align with the principles of early childhood education and personal development. Building and nurturing relationships is paramount to me; I prioritise trust and open communication among team members. I value creating an enjoyable workplace, knowing that a positive environment fosters creativity* *and growth. By setting clear goals and sharing them with my team, we focus our efforts and work collaboratively towards achieving our shared objectives.*

–Jessica

These philosophies and conceptualisations are characterised by transformational and generative leadership. The philosophies are distinguished by effective communication, ongoing professional growth, personal development, visionary thinking and innovation. All value a strengths-based approach in teams and a commitment to others' development. The philosophies align with the findings on leadership in effective settings (Coleman et al., 2016; Siraj-Blatchford & Manni, 2007), and these undergraduates are on track to work collaboratively and deliver high-quality ECEC for children and families.

Conclusion

Leadership emergence and development are anchored in understandings and conceptualisations of leadership theory and practice. This chapter, therefore, encouraged you to think differently about leadership and explore conceptualisations of leadership theory over time. New conceptualisations will, however, always be foregrounded by historical thinking and theoretical accounts of traditional leadership. New thinking on leadership theory and practices, however, demands different approaches to development that move beyond investing power in individuals and the hope that charisma will carry positional leaders along with followers to achieve great goals. Alternative conceptualisations also require different thinking on the skills, knowledge and values that are required for emerging and positional leaders. The next chapter, therefore, delves into the complex knowledge, skills and values significant to ECEC leadership.

Reflective questions

What theories inform your leadership?

Write a reflective piece on your leadership philosophy as informed by theory.

How can you encourage other team members to develop a leadership philosophy?

References

Aubrey, C., Godfrey, R. & Harris, A. (2013). How do they manage? An investigation of early childhood leadership. *Educational Management Administration & Leadership, 41*(1), 5–29. https://doi.org/10.1177/1741143212462702

Bøe, M. & Hognestad, K. (2015). Directing and facilitating distributed pedagogical leadership: Best practices in early childhood education. *International Journal of Leadership in Education, 20*(2), 133–148. https://doi.org/10.1080/13603124.2015.1059488

Bolman, L. & Deal, T. (2013). *Reframing organizations: Artistry, choice, and leadership* (5th ed.). Wiley.

Brownlee, J., Nailon, D. & Tickle, E. (2010). Constructing leadership in child care: Epistemological beliefs and transformational leadership. *Australasian Journal of Early Childhood, 35*(3), 95–104. https://doi.org/10.1177/183693911003500312

Coleman, A., Sharp, C., & Handscomb, G. (2016). Leading highly performing children's centres. *Educational Management Administration & Leadership, 44*(5), 775–793. https://doi.org/10.1177/1741143215574506

Contractor, N., Dechurch, L., Carson, J., Carter, D. & Keegan, B. (2012). The topology of collective leadership. *The Leadership Quarterly, 23*(6), 994–1011. https://doi.org/10.1016/j.leaqua.2012.10.010

Davis, K., Krieg, S. & Smith, K. (2015). Leading otherwise: Using a feminist-poststructuralist and postcolonial lens to create alternative spaces for early childhood educational leaders. *International Journal of Leadership in Education, 18*(2), 131–148. https://doi.org/10.1080/13603124.2014.943296

Douglass, A. (2018). Redefining Leadership: Lessons from an Early Education Leadership Development Initiative. *Early Childhood Education Journal, 46*(4), 387–396. https://doi.org/10.1007/s10643-017-0871-9

Douglass, A. (2019). Leadership for quality early childhood education and care. *OECD Education Working Paper* (No. 211). OECD Publishing. https://doi.org/10.1787/6e563bae-en

Drucker, P. & Wartzman, R. (2010). *The Drucker lectures: Essential lessons on management, society, and economy*. McGraw Hill.

Dunlop, A. (2008). *A literature review on leadership in the early years*. Learning and Teaching Scotland. Website archived 6 April 2011: https://web.archive.org/web/20110406050458/http:/www.ltscotland.org.uk/publications/a/leadershipreview.asp?strReferringChannel=&strReferringPageID=tcm:4-623087-64

Fisher, C. M., Amabile, T. & Pillemer, J. (2021). How to help (without micromanaging). *Harvard Business Review*, January–February 2021. https://hbr.org/2021/01/how-to-help-without-micromanaging

Gibbs, L. (2022). Leadership emergence and development: Organizations shaping leading in early childhood education. *Educational Management Administration & Leadership, 50*(4), 672–693. https://doi.org/10.1177/1741143220940324

Gibbs, L. (2024). Leading through crisis and complexity. *BELMAS Annual Conference, Glasgow*.

Gibbs, L., Press, F. & Wong, S. (2019). Complexity leadership theory: A framework for leading in Australian early childhood education settings. In P. Strehmel, J. Heikka,

E. Hujala, J. Rodd & M. Waniganayake (Eds), *Leadership in early education in times of change: Research from five continents* (pp. 173–186). Verlag Barbara Budrich.

Heikka, J., Waniganayake, M. & Hujala, E. (2013). Contextualizing distributed leadership within early childhood education: Current understandings, research evidence and future challenges. *Educational Management Administration & Leadership, 41*(1), 30–44. https://doi.org/10.1177/1741143212462700

Hills, L. (2012). *Lasting female educational leadership: Leadership legacies of women leaders.* Springer.

Hujala, E., Eskelinen, M., Keskinen, S., Chen, C., Inoue, C., Matsumoto, M., & Kawase, M. (2016). Leadership tasks in early childhood education in Finland, Japan, and Singapore. *Journal of Research in Childhood Education, 30*(3), 406–421. https://doi.org/10.1080/02568543.2016.1179551

Jung, J.-H. (2004). *Transformational leadership in early childhood education: A study of three Korean early childhood organisations* [Doctoral dissertation, Teachers College, Columbia University]. ProQuest Dissertations Publishing. https://www.proquest.com/openview/4375d28cbfe7b5f8f62a9cae7c0c4e83/1?pq-origsite=gscholar&cbl=18750&diss=y

Kemmis, S., Wilkinson, J., Edwards-Groves, C., Hardy, I., Grootenboer, P., & Bristol, L. (2014). Praxis, Practice and Practice Architectures. In S. Kemmis, J. Wilkinson, C. Edwards-Groves, I. Hardy, P. Grootenboer, & L. Bristol (Eds.), *Changing practices, changing education.* (pp. 25–41). Springer.

Klevering, N. & McNae, R. (2018). Making sense of leadership in early childhood education: Tensions and complexities between concepts and practices. *Journal of Educational Leadership, Policy and Practice, 33*(1), 5–17. https://doi.org/10.21307/jelpp-2018-002

Li, Y. (2015). The culture of teacher leadership: A survey of teachers' views in Hong Kong early childhood settings. *Early Childhood Education Journal, 43*(5), 435–445. https://doi.org/10.1007/s10643-014-0674-1

Liew, J. (2017). *A Systematic Review on Strategies for Leadership Development in the Early Childhood Sector–Applicability to the Singapore Context.* https://eppi.ioe.ac.uk/cms/Portals/0/PDF%20reviews%20and%20summaries/Joanna%20Liew_Dissertation.pdf?ver=2019-01-11-140552-583

Marion, R. (2008). Complexity Theory for Organizations and Organizational Leadership. In M. Uhl-Bien & R. Marion (Eds.), *Complexity Leadership Part 1: Conceptual Foundations.* Information Age Publishing, Inc.

Marion, R., & Gonzales, L. (2013). *Leadership in education: Organizational theory for the practitioner.* Waveland Press.

Mettiäinen, V. (2016). Early childhood education teachers and leaders becoming the leadership(s). *Reconceptualizing Educational Research Methodology, 7*(2), 62–73. https://doi.org/10.7577/rerm.1842

Muijs, D., Aubrey, C., Harris, A. & Briggs, A. (2004). How do they manage?: A review of the research on leadership in early childhood. *Journal of Early Childhood Research, 2*(2), 157–169. https://doi.org/10.1177/1476718X04042974

Nicolini, D. (2012). *Practice theory, work, and organization: An introduction.* Oxford University Press.

O'Neill, C., & Brinkerhoff, M. (2018). *Five elements of collective leadership*. Redleaf Press.

Raelin, J. A. (2016). *Leadership-as-practice: Theory and application*. Routledge.

Raelin, J. A. (2018). What are you afraid of: Collective leadership and its learning implications. *Management Learning, 49*(1), 59–66. https://doi.org/10.1177/1350507617729974

Rodd, J. (2013). *Leadership in early childhood: The pathway to professionalism* (4th ed.). Allen & Unwin.

Sarros, J. C. & Santora, J. C. (2001). The transformational-transactional leadership model in practice. *Leadership & Organization Development Journal, 22*(8), 383–394. https://doi.org/10.1108/01437730110410107

Sinclair, A. (2008). *Leadership for the disillusioned: Moving beyond myths and heroes to leading that liberates*. Allen & Unwin.

Siraj-Blatchford, I., & Manni, L. (2007). *Effective leadership in the early years sector: The ELEYS study*. Institute of Education Press.

Spillane, J. P. (2012). *Distributed leadership* (Vol. 4). Wiley & Sons.

Stamopoulos, E. & Barblett, L. (2018). *Early childhood leadership in action: Evidence-based approaches for effective practice*. Allen & Unwin.

Stewart, J. (2006). Transformational leadership: An evolving concept examined through the works of Burns, Bass, Avolio, and Leithwood. *Canadian Journal of Educational Administration and Policy, 54*. https://journalhosting.ucalgary.ca/index.php/cjeap/issue/view/2936

Tucker, D. (2019). *Characteristics of successful early childhood educational leaders* [Doctoral dissertation, Walden University]. Walden Dissertations and Doctoral Studies. https://scholarworks.waldenu.edu/dissertations/7204

Uhl-Bien, M. & Arena, M. (2017). Complexity leadership: Enabling people and organizations for adaptability. *Organizational Dynamics, 46*(1), 9–20. https://doi.org/10.1016/j.orgdyn.2016.12.001

Uhl-Bien, M. & Marion, R. (2007). *Complexity leadership: Part 1: Conceptual foundations*. Information Age Publishing Inc.

Waniganayake, M., Cheeseman, S., Fenech, M., Hadley, F. & Shepherd, W. (2023). *Leadership: Contexts and complexities in early childhood education* (3rd ed.). Oxford University Press.

Wilkinson, J. (2017). Leading as a socially just practice: Examining educational leading through a practice lens. In K. Mahon., S. Francisco & S. Kemmis (Eds), *Exploring education and professional practice* (pp. 165–182). Springer.

Wilkinson, J. & Kemmis, S. (2014). Practice theory: Viewing leadership as leading. *Educational Philosophy and Theory, 47*(4), 342–358. https://doi.org/10.1080/00131857.2014.976928

Wilkinson, J., Olin, A., Lund, T., Ahlberg, A., & Nyvaller, M. (2010). Leading praxis: Exploring educational leadership through the lens of practice architectures. *Pedagogy, Culture and Society, 18*(1), 67–79. https://doi.org/10.1080/14681360903556855

Wilson, J., North, M., Morris, D. & McClellan, R. (2020). Rethinking implicit leadership theories: Tomorrow's leaders are collective, generative, and adaptive. *Journal of Leadership Studies, 14*(3), 24–32. https://doi.org/10.1002/jls.21707

PART

Complexity

Complexity: the state of being complex / complicated and interrelated parts

> *I can draw on leadership styles, theories and implement tools such as critical conversation frameworks to support my role in the trickier situations as well as my own personal lived experience. What I do find challenging in the Early Childhood Profession is the emotional drain that is often placed on the leader. Often you can be the sounding board for families and staff about matters affecting families and relationships. Ensuring you put in place clear work boundaries-how and when you can be contacted outside work times and ensuring that when changes or new procedures/policies are implemented that they care communicated clearly and effectively.*
> —Rhonda, educational professional and leader for 20 years, Study 2

DOI: 10.4324/9781003277590-5

Cultivating Leadership in Early Childhood Education and Care

We must aim for better high quality for children, for families, for us. We expect more than the minimum. I think it's not the minimum because it's a quality standard, but I think we've been working to that, and I want more.

I want influence with each other, I want influence in the community, I want it horizontally, vertically. I want it both ways and downwardly. You know, upwards and downwards and when we're working with diverse communities and diverse communities of educators, let alone communities of clients and children, we have to be very skilful to navigate those places, you know, 'as a leader, how much can I push, how much can I listen, learn?'

–Louise, educational professional and
leader for 40 years, Study 1

Dispositions for Leading
Knowledge, Skills, Values

This chapter

- highlights the characteristics of dispositions
- asks 'What is my leadership for?'
- defines the concept of leader dispositions made up of skills, knowledge and values
- looks at leadership dispositions through the eyes of leaders and educators
- considers the leader for the future.

Introduction

According to Kemmis et al. (2014), dispositions are shaped by knowledge, skills and values. These elements are evident in the sayings, doings and relatings which are characteristic of a discipline's practices. As emerging and positional leaders immerse themselves in their practices, their dispositions are shaped and reshaped within the rich environment of early childhood education and care (ECEC) organisations.

This chapter explores the skills, knowledge and values that are present and needed for emerging and positional leaders within ECEC to enact leadership effectively. The intention of this book is to argue for leadership development as an organisational responsibility that goes beyond the individual, but it is essential to understand what characterises an effective leader and their practices. The evidence for the unique knowledge, skills and values that make up leader dispositions is drawn from the three studies (and predominantly Studies One and Three) introduced in the Prologue and described in the Appendix.

DOI: 10.4324/9781003277590-6

Cultivating Leadership in Early Childhood Education and Care

The chapter goes on to discuss disruptions to the leadership story, specifically what educators consider a 'good' leader and what a 'good' leader is in ECEC according to empirical research. A narrative begins here on cultivating skills, knowledge and values for both leading and leadership as a practice. Leader profiles, within a framework of knowledge, skills and values, are embedded within this chapter. The chapter begins with stories of coming to leadership and belonging to the profession.

Stories of becoming and belonging

In my first leadership role, I worked with a huge team of early childhood teachers, which I think makes a massive difference. I was only twenty-six, and I don't know how many times I cried in the bathroom because I had no idea what to do with anything that arrived in the post. I could barely turn a computer on. Clearly not great at it!

So, you know, the learning curve was like this. But I was fortunate to work with amazing staff who were forthright. It really taught me a lot about leadership and how to work with the team. I moved to a professional development and advocacy role, but I felt like I should be 'practising what I preach'. I had been out of face-to-face teaching for six and a half years. Absolutely loved it and rediscovered that, you know, I still love teaching. I love being with the children, love that daily interaction with families.

–Sara, Study 2

I have actually been—I have been in early childhood my entire career. I left as a high school student wanting to go into the field. My mom was also a preschool teacher. And I just really loved it. I always had that interest and passion of going to her work and pursued it as well. I have done it; I essentially did my last practicum and took up a job at the same service. And was there for 12 years. And then, I ended up joining the management committee where my son was, and one thing led to another, and I ended up the director at that preschool. I started off as an early childhood teacher, I did some acting

58

Dispositions for Leading

> *director roles when stuff—when the current director sort of went on maternity leave. And there was this natural sort of progression into a late, more leadership sort of role. And I probably did about five years of teaching. I really enjoy the multifaceted sort of approach. I guess what inspires me about the staff, the children, the families in the community that that we work so closely with and obviously the service provision. I am quite passionate and dedicated. I think colleagues would say that I'm sort of calm and approachable and friendly. But an extremely high achiever. I have high expectations as a leader, I suppose. And sometimes I guess people can struggle to keep up sometimes. They often describe as being a few steps ahead. So sometimes people are so playing catch up, I suppose. But I didn't have any formal training as a leader.*
>
> –Kim, Study 2

What is my leadership for?

There is an increasing focus on leadership in ECEC. Chapter 2 highlighted conceptualisations of leadership and a transition to practices of leading. Such a transition creates an opportunity for collective approaches to leadership, but at the heart of the issue is the question *What is my leadership for?* This question unleashes a complex array of responses. Is the practice of leading in ECEC to create equality? To nurture citizenship? To supply profits for the corporations who deliver ECEC? To mentor educators to prepare children for formal schooling?

Sinclair (2008) challenges the conventional wisdom and myths about leadership that have dominated the leadership discourse. She questions the purpose and the outcomes of leadership that are based on assertiveness, confidence, control and heroism. Sinclair argues that such leadership is often driven by narrow interests, ego and fear and that it fails to address the complex and interconnected challenges of the contemporary world.

These complex and interconnected challenges are ever present in the sites of ECEC as positional leaders respond to complicated policy and funding regimes, evolving theory and ECEC practice, workforce precarity, child and family profiles, complex industrial relations landscapes, human resource management and increasing demands from ongoing crises of pandemics and climate disasters (Alchin et al., 2019; Gibbs et al., 2019, Quinones et al., 2023). The question on the purpose of ECEC leadership influences the response to this complexity and shapes pathways to and cultivation of leadership.

So, what is early childhood leadership for? Is leadership for social justice and advocacy, child development, growth of citizens of the future, and progress of the profession, development of others and their leadership, workforce sustainability, compliance, educational quality, and profit for shareholders. The underlying intentions of leadership are to shape the pathways to leadership and practices of leading that avoid a leadership ideology described by Sinclair (2008) as "punishing and ultimately unsustainable ways of working and living" (Loc 320). Positional leaders often have had inadequate practice of 'leading' (Sinclair, 2008; Waniganayake et al., 2023). Sinclair (2008) and Waniganayake et al. (2023) maintain that leaders may shape their leadership as a charismatic, individualistic model that is unsustainable for organisations and individuals either within or outside of the ECEC sector. Understanding the central premise for leadership provides a foundation for further development of research and the practice of leading in ECEC.

International research identifies the complex impetuses that drive leaders. For example, leadership is for inspiring and managing people (Alchin et al., 2019; Brooker & Cumming, 2019), aligning compliance and innovation (Gibbs et al., 2019) or balancing economic rationalism with narratives of quality (Halttunen et al., 2019; Nuttall et al., 2020).

The diverse purposes are antecedent to the centralisation of the leadership role. Yet loading up the positional leadership role with duties, tasks and responsibilities for the well-being and progress of the team places great demands and expectations upon a single leader.

There is an established connection between the quality of ECEC environments and effective leadership practices (Douglass, 2019). However, the characteristics of effective leadership still need to be clearly identified and developed in the field. Often, individuals find themselves in formal leadership roles inadvertently rather than through deliberate career planning. Moreover, these leaders frequently lack sufficient experience in 'leading' (Sinclair, 2008; Waniganayake et al., 2023). According to Sinclair (2008) and Waniganayake et al. (2023), such a pattern of leadership is untenable and poses risks to the sustainability of both organisations and individuals, extending beyond the ECEC sector (Gibbs et al., 2019).

Dispositions for Leading

The anticipated growth in ECEC services signals a rising demand for leaders with professional acumen, leadership training, and proficiency. While studies have examined various leadership development programs within ECEC contexts, evidence remains inconclusive regarding their effectiveness in fostering effective leadership in both formal and informal capacities or in enhancing the quality of services (Layen, 2015; Nicholson & Kroll, 2015; Stamopoulos, 2015; Talan et al., 2014). Novice and potential leaders still feel unprepared for leadership enactment (Sims et al., 2014). Standalone personal development initiatives have yet to mitigate these concerns, and the issue of leaders emerging by chance rather than through structured progression persists (Gibbs et al., 2019).

The increasing complexity of the positional leadership role is also concerning. Where more must be done to prepare leaders, the onus of facilitating leadership pathways for all educators falls to the positional leader (Douglass, 2019). This over-reliance on leaders is experienced across the world and poses a critical risk to organisations and leaders themselves. This type of leadership, described as 'single-handed heroism' by Sinclair (2008, Loc. 199), is unsustainable and 'may be bad for leaders, followers and organisations alike, not to mention wider society' (Sinclair, 2008, p. 218). Without mediation, the complex nature of the leadership role itself may result in a lack of educator willingness to take on positional roles of leadership.

The leader and the educator

Despite the unsustainable model of ECEC leadership and the aspiration for collectivity and shared leadership, the primary focus of leadership development remains on the individual leader and the best methods for upskilling that individual. Studies have focused on programs of leadership development (e.g., Stamopoulos, 2015; Thornton & Cherrington, 2014; Rodd, 2013), and questions remain about how to best prepare ECEC leaders for the complex and unpredictable challenges of the role and how to 'grow' leadership.

This challenge, to grow professional leaders, was exacerbated during the pandemic in the early 2020s. Instead of government and communities focusing on the professional role that ECEC educators and leaders were playing, there was an intensification of the 'feminised' model of ECEC. This positioning of educators and ECEC leaders, secured in a historical narrative, was exaggerated by the role these educators played during the pandemic.

According to Quinones et al. (2023), leaders and educators were described as 'Covid Warriors' by communities as they created new teaching and learning environments. In many countries, remote teaching replaced face-to-face teaching, while in others, such as Australia, there were intermittent lockdowns and interruptions to teaching norms. Given the play-based nature of preschool teaching and learning activities in most countries, educators had to reimagine the relationships and pedagogical practices in everyday teaching and learning contexts.

The pandemic highlighted the inequalities in the ECEC sector. Ebrahim et al. (2021) drew attention to how the socially advantaged ECEC organisations and settings forged ahead with digital learning, professional development and leadership support, while the socially disadvantaged contexts struggled to meet the demands of the 'new normal'. Koen et al. (2021) noted that the lack of resources, psychosocial support, informative guidelines about Covid-19 protocols and parental support widened the education gap between young children from advantaged and disadvantaged contexts.

Despite the challenges, teachers and leaders across contexts showed extraordinary resilience as they attempted early learning continuity in a crisis. Quinones et al. (2023) explored the emotional demands experienced by ECEC educators in Australia during ongoing periods of lockdown. The findings showcased the ECEC educators' struggle for recognition and how solidarity among educators emerged as a critical response. The implications of the study provide an impetus to actively recognise the early childhood profession.

The pandemic also highlighted the need for leaders in ECEC to be resilient and adaptable in the face of uncertainty. Early childhood leaders settled into a pattern of supporting educator well-being, establishing trust, ensuring safety, including educators' voices and empowering them to make choices that improved both their teaching and children's learning environments that may have been online.

The pandemic emphasised the importance of adaptability, flexibility and resilience in uncertain times. It also highlighted the need for leaders in ECEC to prioritise the well-being of educators and children while maintaining social connections and providing quality education. Further difficulty exists when considering how to prepare leaders for the challenges faced not only during times of crisis but also in the complex everyday 'happenings' within an ECEC setting.

Dispositions for Leading

Additionally, the pandemic pushed emerging and positional leaders to question their own skills and confidence, as Loretta describes below. There has been inadequate support for rebuilding organisations and personal efficacy post pandemic.

> *I feel I am lacking confidence after the past few years of being in a few different services, moving from smaller owner-operated to a big organisation and with the pandemic I sort of 'lost myself' as a teacher. I feel I have strong knowledge of early childhood and with my many years of experience I have a lot to offer. My experience with coaching/mentoring helped me greatly in exploring my capacities of being a leader and helping other people build on their own confidence and capacities as educators. I am confident in my work as a teacher, but I can be insecure about my own personality. I can come across as too confident or assertive to others and I often doubt myself in case my tone is not right and am hyper-aware of how I come across to others constantly.*
>
> *I'm in a bit of a 'funk' and forgetting my own capacities and passions and I think to get back into leadership and helping other people finding their strengths, I need to find my own again first and I hope to gain clarity, knowledge, confidence and strength.*
>
> –Loretta, Study 2

ECEC leadership dispositions: Practice or position?

A step towards developing people is to first understand the skills and knowledge required for the practice of leading and, subsequently, the positional role of leadership in ECEC. An important consideration is the 'dispositions' exemplified by ECEC professionals as they lead.

A common definition of disposition refers to a person's quality of mind and character. Other definitions encompass values, commitment and professional ethics. Dispositions can also be narrowly applied to a leader's character and capacity to show empathy towards those people they lead (Crossan et al., 2015). Dispositions are defined here through the lens of the theory of practice architectures (a further brief explanation of the theory of practice architectures appears in Chapter 5), where dispositions are comprised of knowledge, skills and values exemplified in the practices of leading (Kemmis et al., 2014). This definition aims to reposition the framing of the ECEC leader or emerging leader—who is constrained by the socio-cultural view of the ECEC professional—as a saviour, as selfless and as embodying feminine traits of caring and nurturing.

Knowledge, skills and values, evident in 'sayings,' 'doings' and 'relatings', make up these dispositions and are informed by the practices that are characteristic of the discipline of ECEC. By participating in the discipline of ECEC, dispositions are transformed in a dynamic environment where others practice leading. Knowledge, skills and values hang together in the practising or enactment of a practice in which they are relevant and play a part (Kemmis et al., 2014). Through this theoretical lens,

Knowledge is described as forms of understanding embodied in cognitive knowledge, thinking and perceptions that are the foundation of 'sayings'.
Skills describe the modes of action and capabilities in carrying out practices ('doings').
Values describe relating to others and the world ('relatings').

Leary and Tangney (2011) note that the way we perceive ourselves, our self-concept and identity are core to leadership effectiveness. Table 3.1 contains the reflections of three ECE leaders who participated in Study 2 on their knowledge, skills and values. Naomi, Kim and Kerrie identified their perceptions of the knowledge, skills and values they possess that support their work as leaders. These reflections are shared to demonstrate their understandings of their own dispositions in the context of their practices.

Reflective questions

How can these leaders' accounts of knowledge, skills and values inform your practice of leading?
What are your knowledge, skills and values that support your work as a leader or emerging leader?

The entangled knowledge, skills and values

A comprehensive repertoire of knowledge, skills and values, such as those documented in Table 3.1, is evident in leadership practices (Gibbs, 2020,

Table 3.1 Self-perception of knowledge, skills and values (Study 2)

	Naomi	Kim	Kerrie
Knowledge	Knowledge of regulations and standards, knowledge of role of nominated supervisor, knowledge of all staff roles, knowledge of policies and philosophy, knowledge of child development.	Effective communication and delegation are key to effectively leading the service. Considering various perspectives and respecting key stakeholders affords making informed decisions.	'I have knowledge of different leadership types and the need to adapt and change to these styles depending on whom I am leading. I understand the importance of a leading by example and role modelling expectations.'
Skills	Effective communicator and listener, put staff well-being at forefront of decisions, take on responsibility of nominated supervisor, have a shared vision with the team and management committee, value family input, encourage others to share their passions, good analytical person.	Qualifications: early childhood teacher qualification, Advanced Diploma in Community Sector Management, Certificate IV in Assessment and Training, ongoing Professional Development, Mental Health First Aider, Leadership courses. Dispositions: empathy, self-awareness, courage, curiosity, creativity, respect, gratitude, integrity and a sense of humour! Skills: learning agility, communication, professional, ethical, influence/respect, values/beliefs. Knowledge/experience: in sector nearly 30 years, worked in multiple service types, ongoing professional development, keeps self up-to-date with changes, mindful leadership, networking, collaborative approach.	'I have a clear visions and philosophies which ensure that I can lead my team to provide quality care and education. I am extremely committed to my career and expectations of my leadership position. I am enthusiastic in ensuring that I meet the needs of my team and encourage open and respectful communication. I understand that leadership can be complex and there is a constant need for reflection and change dependent on what is happening within my team.'

(Continued)

Table 3.1 (Continued)

	Naomi	Kim	Kerrie
Values	Empathy towards others, kindness to others, generous, willing to share knowledge with others, set a tone of the values, willing to empower others, passion for high early childhood education, diligent worker, lead by example.	Trust and respect, emotional intelligence, patience, accountability, empathy and compassion, resilience, communication, collaboration, empowerment and belief in others, learn from mistakes.	'I am flexible and can adapt my leadership style to meet the needs of individuals and varying situations. I value diversity and the differing skills each person brings to the team. I am a good listener and take time to acknowledge my team and listen to their feedback and where needed make changes to ensure everyone is happy.'

Dispositions for Leading

2022). Emerging leaders in ECEC must, therefore, be equipped with an array of interpersonal, organisational and pedagogical skills.

Coleman et al. (2016) note that knowledge manifests through a profound understanding of child development theories, curriculum design and teaching strategies. Leaders must exhibit a mastery of ECEC research and translate theoretical insights into actionable practices that enhance learning outcomes for both children and educators. In a field marked by constant evolution, leaders must also exhibit a propensity for continuous learning and embrace emerging trends and innovative methodologies. Emerging and positional leaders also consider knowledge of the historical traditions of the field to be important.

> *I need historical knowledge of the early childhood sector development knowledge of management and operation of various organisations, knowledge of working with and amongst people with various styles of work, knowledge of different leadership styles to suit various teams of people, knowledge of self and how this is reflected in these models of leadership.*
>
> —Cerise, Study 2

A complex range of skills is required to lead in ECEC settings, including the capacity to deal with boards of directors; committees of management; funding mechanisms; industrial relations arrangements and the mentoring of staff, along with knowledge of child development and pedagogy (Australian Productivity Commission, 2014). Additionally, skills of relationship management are critical, along with the capacity to make decisions that uphold the rights of children, families and educators while effectively running an organisation with financial and governance imperatives (Gibbs, 2022). However, as Nicholson and Kroll (2015) note and Kerrie highlights below, leaders report an intermingling of skills and values.

> *I believe with my years of experience and professional development I have the required knowledge to lead a team successfully. I have a clear visions and philosophies which ensure that I can lead my team to provide quality care and education. I am extremely committed to*

> *my career and expectations of my leadership position. I am passionate in ensuring that I meet the needs of my team and encourage open and respectful communication. I understand that leadership can be complex and there is a constant need for reflection and change dependent on what is happening within my team.*
>
> *–Kerrie, Study 2*

Central to the leadership narrative is the cultivation of values that resonate with the core principles of ECEC. Ethical considerations, cultural sensitivity and a commitment to inclusivity must permeate a leader's actions and decisions. These values serve as a compass guiding leaders through the moral dilemmas and intricate choices that arise in their journey. Continuing reflection on values as a team also shapes and enables leadership. As Kim notes below, values are critical to her practice as a leader.

> *My values are crucial to me as a person and as a leader. My values are part of who I am and how I live my life. My values keep be grounded and support me in decision making. I'm also conscious that people have different values and beliefs.*
>
> *–Kim, Study 2*

What did the three studies tell us about dispositions made up of knowledge, skills and values?

The expression of disposition through practices is illustrated in the three studies of emerging and positional leaders described in the Prologue. Common to all emerging and positional leaders in the three studies was the *knowledge* demonstrated within responsive decision-making and discipline language. In all three studies, emerging and positional leader decision-making and language were informed by cognitive understandings of children's development along with regulation, policy and learning frameworks. Emerging and positional leaders also actively updated their knowledge of quality standards:

Dispositions for Leading

> *The knowledge I have to be a leader I've attained over a significant period of time through study, research, a variety of interesting professional experiences, creating opportunities for myself to learn and grow and working in a multitude of leadership roles in education. My knowledge has evolved over time, developing into a sense of wisdom, and understanding.*
>
> –Kim, Study 2

Emerging and positional leaders also actively participated in professional development to enrich their practice. All strongly agreed that they had a sound understanding of the governance of their organisations. This understanding was key to navigating systems and processes. Additionally, risks in pedagogical decision-making were informed by deep understandings of the policy landscape and traditions of ECEC. For example, *The Flag Project* (below) illustrates this risk-taking in engaging in complex topics with children informed by the social justice tradition within ECEC. In this instance, socially just practice is exemplified by educators' and leaders' deep respect for First Nations history and culture.

The Flag Project began with the question, 'Why do we have four flag poles but only three flags?' and led to a flag-raising ceremony almost nine months later. The children wanted to make a symbol of their connection to the place where they spend their days. They insisted on ensuring that not only our school was represented but also the people who came before us, the Aboriginal people. They reflected on their relationship to the land on which we live and play and how they could develop their own symbols to represent their connection. Their respect for this place, their community and the natural world was evident throughout their work. This sense of consideration led to a long research process to understand flags, colour, symbols and meaning. To reflect on this project, I feel immense pride in seeing the 'real life' flag arrive. We did it! This flag represents so much more than our little school on the roof. The children were genuinely considerate of our world when creating this flag.

(Klarissa in Salamon et al., 2024, p. 6)

In the Flag Project example, the interest in children's rights and well-being ensured that leaders prioritised children's agency in their pedagogical decision-making. Conversations, actions and professional language were informed by knowledge from training and qualifications, child protection training, trauma-informed practice training and professional learning. Mentoring and coaching conversations were constructed through in-depth knowledge of the profession and research-informed practice.

Regardless of their qualifications and experience, the *skills* of the emerging leaders in the three studies informing this book were evident as they presented ideas and led conversations in team meetings. Innovative solutions for change and creative ways of working were embedded in their everyday practice, and this is a mark of leading in complex environments (Uhl-Bien & Arena, 2017). All the leaders embraced opportunities to collaborate and contribute equally to pedagogy and decision-making about children and families.

Leaders were also skilled in having 'hard' yet productive conversations and enabling educators' strengths. *Reinvigorating practice* (below) illustrates how one leader used their skills in having hard conversations to strengthen practice.

Reinvigorating practice

Educators were coming to work, and their engagement with the children seem to be getting less and less. Or it wasn't that enthusiastic. I tried a variety of different approaches, having those direct conversations as well as one-on-one. So, we sat together and tried to focus on a strength-based approach. All the educators wrote about what they believe. There's transfer between what they believe, and they were really good at contributing towards the curriculum. And this one particular staff member had written in that—she loves nature so much and her preferred area in our environment was to be outdoors. She said she would love to be given responsibility of the composting and the sustainability and the veggie garden that side. So, we were like, well, okay, you can. You can take that role. And you know, initially, she didn't invite any children up to that area with her to go and help do all these jobs. Obviously, out of curiosity, they naturally gravitated up there. And she eventually that one fuzzy feeling came back to her, and thankfully, now she has come back into the fold.

–Susan, Study 2

Dispositions for Leading

Susan's approach in the *Reinvigorating practice* account demonstrates her skills that she describes as 'vision, patience, great listener, able to steer the ship and rise above challenges ... [a]ble to delegate to ensure that all areas of the business are considered important, while adapting to the market conditions or needs of our families'.

Emerging and positional leaders were also skilled in balancing innovation, change, disruption and compliance (Gibbs, 2022). Skilful practices surrounded the management of funding and regulations. For example, funding and policy guidelines were interpreted by leaders in ways that enabled inclusive practice. Leaders were also adept in promoting cultures of trust and equality. Emerging and positional leaders' practices were shaped by critical reflection and a desire to improve the skills of their practice. Theresa explains below her desire to grow and evolve for her own practice and the well-being of children and families.

As Theresa, an emerging leader, noted,

> *I think it's that constantly wanting to do things better. We talk about greatness, but there is no such thing as greatness. There is, just for me, that drive to want to evolve and make changes and do things better, and how can we evolve this practice, and what can we look at to make things better for ourselves, to have that passion not die for the children and families within our service and for the wider community.*
>
> –Theresa, Study 1

Contextual literacy is the ability to read the situation and take account of the people involved (Siraj-Blatchford & Manni, 2007). Emerging and positional leaders in all three studies confidently navigated the context within the dynamic that was constantly evolving the nature of the organisation.

Emerging and positional leaders' *values* underpinned their actions. Throughout the ECE sites, emerging and positional leaders consistently talked of vision and philosophy as being foundational to their practices of leading. The leaders consistently express a personal alignment with the philosophical principles of the ECEC organisation. Emerging and positional leaders alike innovated, changed and disrupted standard operations to inspire creative approaches to problem solving by, for example, increasing children's access to the outdoors with an excursion pedagogy that included all ages, from babies to five-year-olds. They also enacted their personal values related to social justice and activism.

Emerging and positional leaders' values underpinned their practices. They expressed a personal alignment with the vision and philosophy of the ECEC settings they worked in. All participants showed empathy for families and children. Advocacy actions were linked with the professional identity as an early childhood leader. Advocacy was considered an important responsibility within everyday practice. In this study, socially just leadership practices were observed to be interdependent and constantly reshaping to generate morally informed, purposeful leadership praxis (Palaiologou & Male, 2019).

In conversation: Values

In the research study using the dialogic café method (Study 2), leaders who were asked 'What are the values underpinning your role as a positional leader?' were clear in their responses:

Valuing others: *I think treating everybody how they need to be treated and responded to so that everyone does feel valued.*

–Sara, Study 2

*I would say, valuing the whole team and seeing everyone's worth and acknowledging where they were in their skills and where they've been and where they're going and what they know. We have a value of **celebrating every child**, and I think that extends to our team as well. So, **celebrating everybody's strength in our team**. Their differences, their quirkiness, the way they have fun. Looking at different people's approaches and seeing how that works. So, we can all bring our personality into the team.*

–Rhonda, Study 2

> **Respect**: *I think it makes an enormous difference to children. Families say that genuine respect, and that we actually really like each other. We like to work together. And we make the most out of every day. Covid really made that apparent because it was, she, some days it was really bad, but we kind of all came through it, and we had a good laugh every day.*
>
> –Kim, Study 2

> **Equality**: *I feel that I am respectful, and this would be high on my list of the attributes that a leader must attain. I am fair and listen to my team and value everyone's opinion, skills, knowledge and contributions. I feel passionate about leading by example, and therefore, I would not expect any of my team to undertake a task that I would not do myself.*
>
> –Sara, Study 2

In Study 1, participants were also asked about the attributes they believed were characteristic of effective leaders. These conversations correlate with the research on leadership on effective ECEC sites (e.g., Coleman et al., 2016; Siraj-Blatchford & Manni, 2007). However, other attributes should be considered from a range of perspectives and lead to questions on leadership development. If these attributes, discussed below, are considered important and characteristic of effective leaders, what does this mean for people who are aspiring to positional leadership roles? Are these attributes characteristic of effective leaders, or are they favourable attributes for building relationships? If this is the case, then how do positional leaders manage the expectations of those around them, and where do they focus their efforts for the development of high-quality ECE and programs? How do positional leaders experience these expectations, and how is their well-being affected by them? These questions are important to consider in the development of leadership within the organisation.

Within all three study sites, emerging and positional leaders' dispositions informed their administrative, adaptive and enabling practices (Marion &

Gonzales, 2013). Leadership was rooted in understandings of pedagogical quality, and this concept was supported by the presence of regulations. Yet compliance was balanced with creativity. All educators were empowered in their pedagogical leadership. Leaders harnessed educators' understandings of pedagogy to ensure compliance with ECEC regulations and standards. It was possible to be compliant with the regulations and standards only by activating and enhancing the knowledge and skills of the educators within the setting. The activation of knowledge and skills led to creativity, innovation and the emergence of leading. Collective approaches to leadership facilitated high-quality pedagogy. Within the settings, all educators had a right and responsibility to lead the educational program and practice, not solely those in formal leadership roles. This responsibility prepared educators for formal leadership roles. As Frida, a positional leader, noted,

Regulation has helped us to develop a culture of inquiry-one where we work together for the children. This allows us to keep educational program and professional practice at the centre of our work.

(Gibbs et al., 2019)

A note on the duality of 'effective' leadership

Amidst the tapestry of leadership stories regarding knowledge, skills and values, a perplexing disconnection surfaces: there is a dissonance between educators' perceptions of a 'good' leader and the authentic embodiment of effective leadership in ECEC. The interplay between the idealised notion of leadership and the lived experiences of leaders ultimately reveals the nuances that distinguish a 'good' leader in theory from one in practice.

The narrative about the expectations and characteristics that define the 'good' leader is often at odds with effective practices of leading. Although educators often envision leaders as charismatic figures who possess unwavering confidence and decision-making abilities, it is clear the embodiment of leadership is expressed through the sayings, doings and relatings present in knowledge, skills and values. These practices are also not exclusive to positional leaders; effective leading can be practised by emerging and positional leaders alike.

This takes us back to the starting theme of this chapter: the knowledge, skills and values that are critical to effective leadership practice.

Dispositions for Leading

Enabling and constraining the practices of leading and leadership

If effective leadership is a key factor that influences the quality of ECEC, and indeed that is the goal, it is essential to develop the leadership potential of both emerging and established leaders. Leadership in ECEC is not confined to formal roles or positions but rather involves the knowledge, skills and values that enable educators to work together, innovate and advocate for the best interests of children and families.

There are at least three key reasons why the development of the leadership of all educators in ECEC is important. First, it can strengthen the professional identity and competence of educators, who often encounter difficulties such as low pay, high attrition and lack of recognition. By creating a culture of ongoing learning, reflection and improvement, leaders can empower educators to achieve their goals and aspirations and to deal with the challenges and complexities of their work.

Second, it can enhance the quality and effectiveness of ECEC practices, which rely on the ability of educators to respond to the varied and changing needs of children and families. By establishing a shared vision, values and expectations, organisations can foster collaboration and communication among educators as well as other stakeholders such as parents, community members and policy-makers. Further, by stimulating creativity and innovation, leadership development can motivate educators to try to implement new ideas and methods and to assess and enhance their outcomes.

Third, it can support the advancement and advocacy of ECEC as a field, which often faces difficulties such as low funding, insufficient regulation and marginalisation. By increasing awareness and understanding the importance and impact of ECEC, leaders can affect the attitudes and behaviours of the public and decision-makers to secure support and resources for ECEC. By developing a sense of agency and responsibility, leadership development can enable educators to engage in and influence the policies and practices that affect ECEC.

Conclusion

Developing the leadership knowledge, skills and values of all educators in ECEC is crucial for ensuring the quality and availability of ECEC and for improving the well-being of children and society. Leadership in ECEC is not a static or innate characteristic but rather a dynamic process that can

Cultivating Leadership in Early Childhood Education and Care

be nurtured and supported through various strategies and opportunities. Therefore, it is vital to invest in and prioritise the leadership development of all educators in ECEC, as they are the key agents of change and improvement in ECEC.

Reflective questions and activities

Consider the question: What is my leadership for? Map your thoughts or draw a picture of your motivation and purpose for leading and leadership.

Reflect on your current knowledge, skills and values for leading and leadership.

Reflect on your perceived knowledge, skills and values needed for leading and leadership.

References

Alchin, I., Arthur, L. & Woodrow, C. (2019). Evidencing leadership and management challenges in early childhood in Australia. *Australasian Journal of Early Childhood*, *44*(3), 285–297. https://doi.org/10.1177/1836939119855563

Australian Productivity Commission. (2014). Childcare and Early Childhood Learning, Inquiry Report No. 73, Canberra.

Brooker, M. & Cumming, T. (2019). The 'dark side' of leadership in early childhood education. *Australasian Journal of Early Childhood*, *44*(2), 111–123. https://doi.org/10.1177/1836939119832073

Coleman, A., Sharp, C. & Handscomb, G. (2016). Leading highly performing children's centres: Supporting development of the 'accidental leaders'. *Educational Management Administration & Leadership*, *44*(5), 775–793. https://doi.org/10.1177/1741143215574506

Crossan, M., Seijts, G. & Gandz, J. (2015). *Developing leadership character*. Routledge.

Douglass, A. (2019). Leadership for quality early childhood education and care. *OECD Education Working Paper* (No. 211). OECD Publishing. https://doi.org/10.1787/6e563bae-en

Ebrahim, H. B., Martin, C. & Excell, L. (2021). Early childhood teachers' and managers' lived experiences of the COVID-19 pandemic in South Africa. *Journal of Education (University of KwaZulu-Natal)*, *84*, 204–221. https://doi.org/10.17159/2520-9868/i84a11

Gibbs, L. (2020). "That's your right as a human isn't it?" The emergence and development of leading as a socially-just practice in early childhood education. *Australasian Journal of Early Childhood*, *45*(4), 295–308.

Dispositions for Leading

Gibbs, L. (2022). Leadership emergence and development: Organizations shaping leading in early childhood education. *Educational Management Administration & Leadership, 50*(4), 672–693. https://doi.org/10.1177/1741143220940324

Gibbs, L., Press, F. & Wong, S. (2019). Compliance in a landscape of complexity: Regulation and educational leadership. In L. Gibbs & M. Gasper (Eds), *Challenging the intersection of policy with pedagogy* (pp. 159–174). Routledge.

Halttunen, L., Sims, M., Waniganayake, M., Hadley, F., Bøe, M., Hognestad, K. & Heikka, J. (2019). Working as early childhood centre directors and deputies: Perspectives from Australia, Finland and Norway. In P. Strehmel, J. Heikka, E. Hujala, J. Rodd & M. Waniganayake (Eds), *Leadership in early education in times of change: Research from five continents* (pp. 231–252). Verlag Barbara Budrich.

Kemmis, S., Wilkinson, J., Edwards-Groves, C., Hardy, I., Grootenboer, P. & Bristol, L. (2014). Praxis, practice and practice architectures. In S. Kemmis, J. Wilkinson, C. Edwards-Groves, I. Hardy, P. Grootenboer & L. Bristol (Eds), *Changing practices, changing education* (pp. 25–41). Springer.

Koen, M., Neethling, M. & Taylor, B. (2021). The impact of COVID-19 on the holistic development of young South African at-risk children in three early childhood care and education centres in a rural area. *Perspectives in Education, 39*(1), 138–156. https://doi.org/10.18820/2519593X/pie.v39.i1.9

Layen, S. (2015). Do reflections on personal autobiography as captured in narrated life-stories illuminate leadership development in the field of early childhood? *Professional Development in Education, 41*(2), 273–289. https://doi.org/10.1080/19415257.2014.986814

Leary, M. R. & Tangney, J. P. (2011). The self as an organizing construct in the behavioral and social sciences. In M. R. Leary & J.P. Tangney (Eds), *Handbook of self and identity* (2nd ed., pp. 1–20). Guilford Publications.

Marion, R. & Gonzales, L. (2013). *Leadership in education: Organizational theory for the practitioner*. Waveland Press.

Nicholson, J. & Kroll, L. (2015). Developing leadership for early childhood professionals through oral inquiry: Strengthening equity through making particulars visible in dilemmas of practice. *Early Child Development and Care, 185*(1), 17–43. https://doi.org/10.1080/03004430.2014.903939

Nuttall, J., Henderson, L., Wood, E. & Trippestad, T. (2020). Policy rhetorics and responsibilization in the formation of early childhood educational leaders in Australia. *Journal of Education Policy, 37*(1), 17–38. https://doi.org/10.1080/02680939.2020.1739340

Palaiologou, I. & Male, T. (2019). Leadership in early childhood education: The case for pedagogical praxis. *Contemporary Issues in Early Childhood, 20*(1), 23–34. https://doi.org/10.1177/1463949118819100

Quinones, G., Berger, E. & Barnes, M. (2023). Promoting care for the wellbeing of early childhood professionals in Australia. *Australasian Journal of Early Childhood, 48*(4), 307–318. https://doi.org/10.1177/18369391231202837

Rodd, J. (2013). *Leadership in early childhood: The pathway to professionalism* (4th ed.). Allen & Unwin.

Salamon, A., Gibbs, L., and Cooke, M. (2024) Democratic Practices with and for Our Youngest Citizens: Early Childhood Education, Agency, and the Education Complex in *World Worth Living In (Volume 2)*. Springer.

Sims, M., Forrest, R., Semann, A. & Slattery, C. (2014). Conceptions of early childhood leadership: Driving new professionalism? *International Journal of Leadership in Education, 18*(2), 149–166. https://doi.org/10.1080/13603124.2014.962101

Sinclair, A. (2008). *Leadership for the disillusioned: Moving beyond myths and heroes to leading that liberates*. Allen & Unwin.

Siraj-Blatchford, I. & Manni, L. (2007). *Effective leadership in the early years sector: The ELEYS study*. Institute of Education, University of London.

Stamopoulos, E. (2015). The professional leadership and action research training model: Supporting early childhood leadership. *Australasian Journal of Early Childhood, 40*(4), 39–48. https://doi.org/10.1177/183693911504000406

Talan, T., Bloom, P. J. & Kelton, R. (2014). Building the leadership capacity of early childhood directors: An evaluation of a leadership development model. *Early Childhood Research & Practice, 16*(1&2), Special Section, article 1. https://ecrp.illinois.edu/v16n1/talan.html

Thornton, K. & Cherrington, C. (2014). Leadership in professional learning communities. *Australasian Journal of Early Childhood, 39*(3) 94–102. https://doi.org/10.1177/183693911403900312

Uhl-Bien, M. & Arena, M. (2017). Complexity leadership: Enabling people and organizations for adaptability. *Organizational Dynamics, 46*(1), 9–20. https://doi.org/10.1016/j.orgdyn.2016.12.001

Waniganayake, M., Cheeseman, S., Fenech, M., Hadley, F. & Shepherd, W. (2023). *Leadership: Contexts and complexities in early childhood education* (3rd ed.). Oxford University Press.

The Complex Site of ECEC
Where Leadership Happens

This chapter

- describes ECEC sites as complex systems
- unpacks the complexities of ECEC through the 'education complex'
- examines the implications of complexity for leaders and leadership development.

Introduction

As noted throughout this book, leadership is pivotal in shaping early childhood education and care (ECEC) program quality and outcomes. Regardless of positional and informal roles, effective leadership fosters collaboration, innovation and a shared vision for high-quality ECEC. Yet the emergence and cultivation of leadership are complicated. ECEC organisations are complex, and leadership development and enactment are challenging within that complexity. This chapter describes that complexity to provide a picture of the environment in which leadership evolves and is practiced. An understanding of the environment where leadership is practiced serves as a foundation on which to build leadership development.

ECEC, as a dynamic and multifaceted field, involves diverse stakeholders, contexts and goals. ECEC organisations are not static or isolated entities but rather complex sites that interact with their internal and external environments and evolve over time. This chapter explores ECEC sites as Complex Adaptive Systems (CAS) and the concept of the 'education complex' (Kemmis

DOI: 10.4324/9781003277590-7

Cultivating Leadership in Early Childhood Education and Care

et al., 2014). By using the lens of the education complex, ECEC leaders can critically reflect on the field and address the challenges and opportunities that they face in the complexity of their work. Most importantly, this lens shows the complex ecology of ECEC and its influence on enabling, constraining and shaping leadership.

A story of complexity

I have been working in the EC [early childhood] sector for 29 years—20 of those years in the same community-based preschool as director. Currently, there are 11 staff that work at our service. This has grown from when I started from three. Over this time, I have continued to remain current and reflective to ensure my preschool can deliver and maintain a high quality of education and care within our community. Our service has been through significant challenges going through two major flooding events that have seen our building uninhabitable for over 12 months (we are currently still displaced after the 2022 flooding in northern NSW [New South Wales]). Supporting staff, children and families as well as managing my own well-being, has been immensely difficult. Leaning into the leadership skills that I have helped navigate as best as possible. I work hard to ensure a high morale within our team and support them as much as I can. Sometimes, this is easy and fun; others, it is gut-wrenchingly difficult.

—Karen, Study 2

Karen's story demonstrates the increasing complexity of leading an ECEC organisation. Leadership is performed in ECEC settings in a complex milieu of policy, people and practices with increasingly complicated social dynamics and the effects of political upheaval and global climate disasters, as Karen's story demonstrates. The sites of ECEC and organisations are multifarious. Chapter 3 illuminated the skills, knowledge and values that are needed by emerging and positional leaders. Now, the diverse environment—where leadership happens—is contemplated through an organisational and complexity theory lens.

The Complex Site of ECEC

Organisations and systems

Three perspectives on organisations and complexity are explored: general systems theory (GST), ecological systems theory and CAS theory. These perspectives have shaped thinking in ECEC settings and organisations about operational matters and quality.

General systems theory

Historically, leadership theory and research have been anchored in the belief that organisations adhere to a GST framework. According to GST, as Schneider & Somers (2006) outlined, organisations are characterised by enduring relationship patterns within defined limits. These systems self-regulate through negative feedback to address any imbalance, ensuring the maintenance of their structure and function. The organisation's operation and quality are influenced by external forces, leading to foreseeable and predictable results (Brown, 2011; Schneider & Somers, 2006).

Jorde Bloom (1991), a prominent ECEC leadership scholar, classified 'child care centres' as complex social systems to understand the dynamics of organisational life. Jorde Bloom's systems theory comprised the internal environment (people, structure and processes = internal culture) influenced by the external environment (funding, regulations and professional community). In Jorde Bloom's work, the external environment is cited as a key influence on, but out of the control of, organisations. The external environment includes sponsoring auspicing, regulatory bodies, funding agencies and the professional community (Jorde Bloom, 1991, 2005). In this portrayal, ECEC settings are characterised as products of benevolent external administration. Internal environments, according to Jorde Bloom (1991), are composed of people, structures and processes. People in ECEC settings come together in an intricate web of social networks, values and motivations to form a collective intelligence. Physical and administrative structures guide the activities of individuals in the settings. Processes describe the actions that occur within the structures and are most often conceived and driven by formal leadership. Through this model of systems theory, the formal leader is endowed with the power to direct and guide decision-making to plan, set goals, solve problems, manage conflict and so on (Jorde Bloom, 1991).

81

Ecological systems theory

Bronfenbrenner's ecological systems theory provides a framework for understanding the complex interplay of factors within ECEC. This theory emphasises the significance of multiple environmental systems that affect individuals and focuses on the dynamic interactions within these systems (Härkönnen, 2002; Hayes et al., 2023).

The microsystem, the most immediate and direct level of influence, encompasses the child's immediate environment, such as family, peers and the ECEC setting. In this context, educators play a crucial role in the microsystem, as they directly affect a child's learning and development.

The mesosystem explores the connections between various microsystems. In the context of ECEC, this could involve collaboration between teachers, parents and community resources. Effective communication and collaboration among these components enhance the overall quality of the learning environment.

The exosystem considers broader social structures indirectly influencing the ECEC site, such as local policies, cultural norms and community services. These external factors affect ECEC organisations, and their ability to adapt to societal changes can affect the quality and accessibility of education for young children (Härkönen, 2002).

Finally, the macrosystem encompasses the larger cultural and societal influences on ECEC. These influences include societal values, economic conditions and educational policies at a national level. Policies promoting inclusive and equitable education can positively shape the ECEC landscape and ensure that all children have access to high-quality learning experiences (Hayes et al., 2023).

Complex adaptive systems

CAS theory challenges the traditional GST perspective. CAS suggests that organizations operate in a realm of uncertainty, teetering on the brink of chaos, which is not inherently adverse. Within CAS, interactions are spontaneous and driven by needs and arise organically, acting as catalysts and adapting to feedback. Unlike in GST, where the environment influences outcomes, in CAS, outcomes emerge through direct interaction with the environment. The core tenets of CAS revolve around the system's survival and evolution. Notably, the results of such systems are not predetermined and can lead to unexpected yet potentially beneficial, innovative and creative developments (Gibbs et al., 2019a).

The Complex Site of ECEC

An early explanation of complexity in systems was proposed as an effort to move beyond the narrow meaning and reductionism of GST. Cilliers (1999) asserted that complex systems have characteristics where many elements interact richly in an unpredictable way. The system has feedback loops and exists in a state of disequilibrium.

Marion (2008) maintained that Cilliers (1999) provided this theoretical starting point by capturing the three characteristics of complex systems as interactive, dynamic and adaptive. From there, Marion explored the complex mechanisms that lead to self-organisation, disequilibrium and emergence. Another framing of these principles describes the characteristics of complex systems as decentralised (there is no central control), connected (all elements have a relationship to each other) and co-evolutionary (emergence comes as a natural phenomenon) (Carmody-Bubb, 2023). The application of these principles in systems brings us to the conceptualisation of organisations as CAS.

This is an important feature and an inconsistency when locating ECEC settings within a complexity theory (such as CAS). Complexity theory, conversely, invests power and influence in internal environments. It sees organisations as a creation of the influence and power of internal forces (Hazy & Uhl-Bien, 2015; Marion, 2008).

ECEC organisational theory, such as Jorde Bloom's systems theory and the ecological perspective, have common ground with the principles of both GST and CAS theory (Härkönen, 2002; Waniganayake et al., 2023), but there are points of divergence. ECEC organisations are distinguished by dynamic, productive interrelationships. However, formal leaders in ECEC are principally responsible for predictable outcomes, whereas CAS favours emergence and unpredictable outcomes (Marion & Gonzales, 2013).

The ECEC system is characterised by measurable results such as outcomes of quality assessment. Equilibrium within the organisation is seen as a success of leadership. Jorde Bloom (1991) cites the 'barometer of organizational effectiveness' as the outcomes and notes these as 'multidimensional'. While outcomes are difficult to assess, they complete the 'loop of influences' back to the external environment (Jorde Bloom, 1991). Within a traditional framing of ECEC organisations, pinpointing, scrutinising and resolving issues while establishing approaches that guarantee success are essential. Typically, the formal leader orchestrates this procedure and is accountable for the organisation's performance and efficiency. This approach is characterised by authority and governance, drawing upon a conventional bureaucratic leadership model (Drucker & Wartzman, 2010; Gibbs et al., 2019a; Urban, 2008). An alternative view of ECEC settings as dynamic environments, always in a state of flux and needing to be flexible and adaptive (Urban, 2008), contradicts the perspective that settings must be maintained in a delicate balance to be effective.

This is where CAS can be helpful in understanding the complex environment of ECEC. CAS are entities composed of interconnected and interdependent parts that adapt and evolve in response to changes in their environment. Here is a quick exercise in breaking down the characteristics of ECEC organisations in the context of the CAS literature. ECEC organisations (settings and larger management structures) are characterised by the following:

1. Diverse components: ECEC organisations consist of diverse elements, including teachers, educators, children, administrators and management, family members, learning and programming resources and physical settings. Each of these components influences the overall functioning of the organisation.
2. Interconnectedness: These components are interconnected, meaning they interact with each other in several ways. For example, educators interact with children, parents communicate with administrators, and learning resources inform teaching strategies. Changes in one component can have flow-on effects throughout the organisation.
3. Non-linearity: CAS do not follow linear cause-and-effect relationships. Instead, small changes in one part of the system can lead to disproportionately large and unpredictable effects elsewhere. For example, a new pedagogical method brought to the setting by a new teacher might influence the entire pedagogy within the organisation.
4. Adaptation: ECEC organisations are constantly adapting to changing circumstances. This adaptation can be observed in responses to new educational policies, shifts in family demographics, evolving pedagogies and changes to physical settings or socio-economic circumstances. Organisations must adapt in order to remain effective and relevant.
5. Emergent properties: CAS often exhibit emergent properties, which are characteristics or behaviours that emerge from the interactions of their components. In an ECEC organisation, emergent properties include the overall learning culture, the quality of education provided or the sense of community among children, families, educators, the community and the broader profession.

The Complex Site of ECEC

6. Feedback loops: Feedback loops are mechanisms through which information about the system's performance is transmitted and used to make adjustments. In ECEC, feedback loops can involve assessments of children, teacher and educator evaluations, and family feedback. These loops help the organisation learn and adapt.
7. Self-organisation: CAS have the capacity for self-organisation, meaning they can reconfigure themselves without central control. In ECEC organisations, teachers, educators and administrators may collaboratively change teaching methods, curriculum choices and room dynamics based on their collective experiences and insights.
8. Sensitivity to initial conditions: CAS are often sensitive to initial conditions, meaning that slight differences in starting conditions can lead to significantly different outcomes. This sensitivity is evident in ECEC when considering factors such as the background and experiences of individual students and the initial pedagogical approaches used by teachers and educators.
9. Co-evolution: ECEC organisations co-evolve with their external environment, which includes changes in educational policies, societal values, technology and parental expectations. These external factors can shape the organisation's structure and practices.

ECEC organisations are CAS consisting of diverse and interconnected components that continually adapt and evolve in response to internal and external changes. Recognising them as CAS can help educators and administrators better understand and navigate the dynamic nature of these organisations, fostering a more effective teaching and learning environment (Gibbs et al., 2019b). This is also the environment where leadership is practiced, and by acknowledging the complexity, organisations can commit to sustainable leadership development that does not impose unreasonable expectations upon the individual.

Reflective question

Reflect on the complexity of early childhood organisations and ECEC settings. Note down the components of that complexity in your own setting and organisation.

Unpacking the complexity of the ECEC site

The next step here is to 'unpack' the "complex landscape comprising complicated legislation, a volatile workforce, comprehensive standards of practice and a diversity of children and families" (Gibbs et al., 2019a, p. 174). A complexity lens framework is a method for understanding the evolution of leadership within a setting that encourages educators to engage in leadership practices. This framework fosters an environment conducive to nurturing and enhancing leadership qualities and encourages experimentation and creativity (Gibbs et al., 2019a). Leadership does not occur in isolation, so the influences that shape leadership require deep consideration. This broad unpacking takes into account the jurisdiction, the broader sector and profession, governance structures and the ECEC sites (see Figure 4.1).

The early childhood setting, as a site, has its own ecosystem of educators and staff with a complex array of qualifications and experience, families with varied and diverse needs, pedagogical practices, physical structures and environments, and beyond the walls of an organisation, a community where the setting is situated (Gibbs et al., 2019a; Gibbs & Press, 2023).

At the next level, ECEC organisations are subject to a range of auspices, site management and governance arrangements. Governance arrangements fall into the categories of not-for-profit or for-profit. Not-for-profit services

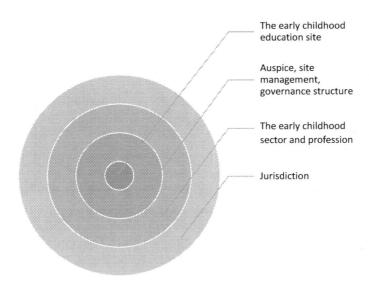

Figure 4.1 The sites of ECEC.

The Complex Site of ECEC

may be governed by local and state government, benevolent societies, faith-based organisations, independent boards, employer organisations (e.g., banks, universities and hospitals) and parent management committees. For-profit services comprise individual owners, franchisers, companies and corporations (Waniganayake et al., 2023).

The ECEC sector and profession also have their own unique characteristics with diversity in how educators come to practice and the traditions and culture of the sector driven (at least initially) by the tenets of social justice and the alleviation of poverty for mothers and children (Kamerman & Gatenio-Gabel, 2007).

Jurisdictional, regulation and monitoring of ECEC vary significantly across countries. Some countries centralise governance under a single ministry, while others decentralise it to regional or municipal administrative authorities.

To further examine this complexity, an analysis of ECEC is carried out through the lens of the education complex (Kemmis et al., 2012). Kemmis et al. (2012) note that practices—in this case, leadership practices—are enabled, constrained and shaped within the ecology of the education complex. This analysis illuminates the conditions in which leading is practised and how the emergence and cultivation of leadership are enabled, constrained and shaped.

ECEC and the education complex

ECEC may include extended day care, pre-school, kindergarten, nursery school, home-based care and preparatory school. Sites not only are important for children's improved cognitive function, health and well-being, school transitions, family connectedness and subsequent access to equitable work and education opportunities but also are places for developing children's interests, culture and inclusion (Organisation for Economic Co-operation and Development [OECD], 2022a). The education complex is a useful lens to tease out the diversity of policy, pedagogy and practice within ECEC showing complexity of the ECEC environment where leaders lead.

The education complex refers to five educational practices that have arisen in response to mass schooling. Similarly, the five interrelated core practices and arrangements emerge in response to the rise of ECEC and the context within which ECEC occurs, but these are expanded with an acknowledgement of the unique model of ECEC. Therefore, the original educational

Cultivating Leadership in Early Childhood Education and Care

practices are identified by Kemmis et al. (2014) as learning practices, teaching practices, professional learning practices, leading practices and researching. These are translated into the ECEC space as children's learning and practice; pedagogy; initial teacher education and professional learning; education policy and administration; leadership, research and quality assessment; and partnerships with families and community (Gibbs & Press, 2023; Salamon et al., 2024). Figure 4.2 identifies the educational practices and demonstrates the relationships between these practices. These elements of the complex within Figure 4.2 are used to unpack the practices within the early childhood environment across several international regions, thus demonstrating the complexity that exists within the field internationally.

The education complex in ECEC varies across jurisdictions and countries worldwide. The education complex is explored below with an example of practices and arrangements in different countries. The examples are not exhaustive but do give an insight into the common and diverse environments where ECEC leading practices are shaped and enacted around the world.

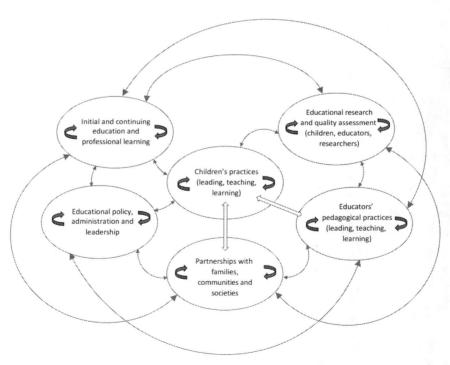

Figure 4.2 The education complex in ECEC (Salamon et al., 2024). Adapted from Kemmis et al. (2012).

The Complex Site of ECEC

Initial teacher and educator preparation and professional learning

Initial teacher and educator preparation refers to the training pathway for people who work in ECEC. Short courses, competency-based training and university degrees are approaches to this preparation. Martha Zaslow (2022), writing for the OECD, notes that early childhood teachers play a leading role in the delivery of ECEC but that there are variations in qualifications across settings. For example, in Japan, the majority of staff working in ECEC are early childhood teachers (around 70%), yet in Australia, only 30% have an early childhood teacher qualification (Izumi-Taylor et al., 2014; Australian Productivity Commission, 2014).

Regional profile | Asia-Pacific | Australia

In Australia, initial early childhood teacher and educator preparation encompasses a range of pathways to prepare for a professional role in ECEC. A Bachelor of Education (Early Childhood) is undertaken in a university as a four-year degree program that encompasses the knowledge, skills and values needed to be effective educators and teachers. Some universities also offer postgraduate degrees (such as master's degrees or postgraduate diplomas) for those with a bachelor's qualification.

Competency-based training emphasises practical skills and competencies required for the role of educator. Educators gain a Diploma or Certificate in Early Childhood through vocational education and training (VET) providers. Educators with a diploma may undertake an accelerated pathway through university to gain a bachelor's degree. A range of short courses train educators and teachers on practical and skill-based aspects of ECEC, such as the Early Years Learning Framework. Training for first aid and child protection is compulsory for all educators. Additionally, teacher registration is a compulsory process for all early childhood teachers, and teachers must meet professional standards of postgraduate professional development and performance. In Australia, there are no formal training requirements for leadership training in ECEC; however, undergraduate courses have compulsory units of study on leading.

Reflective question: How are leadership training and development incorporated into initial teacher and educator preparation and professional learning in your state or country?

89

Educational policy, administration and leadership

Educational policies in ECEC vary significantly from country to country. Some countries prioritise universal access to high-quality early childhood programs (e.g., Finland and Australia), whereas others focus on targeted interventions for disadvantaged children and families. Policy foci include funding, curriculum frameworks, teacher qualifications and assessment practices. Play-based learning, social-emotional development and holistic approaches are prioritised in learning frameworks such as the Te Whāriki of New Zealand.

Administration refers to the governance of an ECEC organisation. Various entities, such as government agencies, local authorities or private organisations, administer ECEC settings. Administrative levers involve licensing, monitoring compliance with regulations and ensuring safety and quality standards. Integration and coordination with the allied health services are common in many countries.

Regional profile | Northern Europe | The Nordic model | Educational policy, administration and leadership

Universal access to education and care is a key feature of the Nordic model of ECEC. The Nordic countries (Denmark, Finland, Iceland, Norway and Sweden) prioritise universal access; for example, children have a right to a place in ECEC in Norway from when they turn one. While the public investment in ECEC is high, there is an increasing provision of services by the private sector, but states continue to play a significant role in ensuring access, quality and affordability. Parental leave policies include generous parental leave, allowing parents to share caregiving responsibilities. This focus on parental involvement shapes ECEC services (Greve & Hansen, 2018). The Nordic model for ECEC strongly emphasises highly trained staff. Educators undergo rigorous training, which ensures their competence in child development, pedagogy and social-emotional support. Additionally, the model promotes an integrated approach, where education and care seamlessly coexist within the same settings. Children from birth to age six often share these environments, and this fosters continuity and community. Collaborative leadership is a characteristic of the Nordic model, in which administrators, teachers and parents actively participate in decision-making. This participatory approach emphasises shared responsibility and democratic principles, and this creates a nurturing and inclusive environment for

The Complex Site of ECEC

young children. For example, there has been a historical emphasis on a flat organisational structure regarding administration and leadership in Swedish preschools. Initially, each preschool teacher held responsibility for administration within their respective preschools. However, in the early 2000s, the role of the preschool manager emerged. These managers primarily focused on administrative tasks and were actively involved in the leading group within the municipality (Lund, 2022).

The Nordic model of quality assurance places significant importance on a holistic curriculum that addresses various dimensions of child development. This includes cognitive, social, emotional and physical aspects. Within this curriculum, play-based learning, creativity and exploration are prioritised. Children engage in activities that foster their overall growth and well-being. The Nordic model prioritises child-centred practices through individualised approaches informed by children's voices.

The continuous professional development model means that educators and leaders engage in ongoing training, reflect on their practices and stay informed about research-based approaches. This commitment to growth is aspirational, as educators aim to provide high-quality care and education (Einarsdottir et al., 2015; Greve & Hansen, 2018).

While public funding for ECEC in the Nordic countries is robust, maintaining quality amid budget constraints remains challenging. Balancing quality and cost-effectiveness requires creative solutions and efficient allocation of resources. Ensuring the retention of skilled staff is an ongoing concern. Burnout and turnover affect the quality of education and care. Strategies such as professional development opportunities, supportive work environments and competitive compensation are crucial. The Nordic model adapts to evolving family structures, migration patterns and societal shifts. Flexibility in program design and responsiveness to diverse family needs are essential (Einarsdottir et al., 2015).

Reflective questions

Are there special initiatives for the development of leadership in educational policy in your state or country?

How do administrative practices support the work of the leader?

Is effective leadership recognised as an important contribution to the quality of ECEC in your state or country, and how is it recognised?

Cultivating Leadership in Early Childhood Education and Care

Educational research and quality assessment (children, educators and researchers)

Educational research focusing on the quality of services and leadership is pivotal in shaping educator practices. Empirical evidence informs teaching and drives positive change. In high-quality ECEC settings, teacher research is actively supported and resourced. Quality standards for ECEC inform practice, raise standards and provide data for accountability and funding (Salamon et al., 2024).

Regional profile | North America | United States | Educational research and quality assessment

ECEC is considered a critical phase that lays the foundation for a child's life-long learning and development, but in the United States, great variation exists in how individual states fund, implement and quality-assure ECEC. The ECEC system in the United States is fragmented, with varying quality and access, and despite recent efforts to integrate, ECEC challenges persist (Hogan, 2019).

Despite the recognition that high-quality ECEC positively affects children, most children in the United States still experience low-quality care (La Paro et al., 2012). The National Association for the Education of Young Children (NAEYC) offers a national, voluntary accreditation system for ECEC programs in the United States. This system sets professional standards to ensure high-quality ECEC experiences for young children. NAEYC accreditation conducts quality assessments of ECE settings, which helps families identify programs that meet rigorous standards, yet only 10,000 settings (around 10 percent of licensed services) engage in the accreditation process (NAEYC, 2024). Advocacy for a more effective, efficient and equitable system of ECEC is carried out by the NAEYC, and this advocacy includes demands for improving education and training levels and economic well-being for early childhood teachers (NAEYC, 2024).

Research and quality assessment in ECEC in the United States involves addressing qualifications improvements and quality, higher education infrastructure, working conditions, remuneration and political advocacy to create a more equitable and effective system. Institutes and private foundations tend to be the predominant actors in research and agents of change. For example, the Early Educator Investment Collaborative (EEIC) envisions a world where every child can access high-quality ECEC programs. The EEIC

The Complex Site of ECEC

works to develop evidence-informed practice where programs are led by well-prepared, well-trained and appropriately compensated early educators. The EEIC collaborates with research partners, including the Center for the Study of Child Care Employment (CSCCE), the National Institute for Early Education Research (NIEER) and Bellwether Education Partners (2020). Their shared vision addresses the ECEC system's intricacies by simultaneously focusing on preparation, working conditions and fair compensation (https://earlyedcollaborative.org/).

Reflective questions

How are leadership and the practices of leading included in standards, curriculum frameworks and quality measures in your state or country?

Is there a program of research that focuses on leadership and quality assurance in your organisation, state or country?

Children's practices (leading, teaching and learning)

Children's practices are shaped by culture, resources and relationships within ECEC settings. Article 31 of the United Nations Convention on the Rights of the Child states that children should have 'the right … to rest and leisure, to engage in play and recreational activities appropriate to the age of the child and to participate freely in cultural life and the arts' (United Nations Children's Fund [UNICEF], 1989, p. 1). Children's practices go on to shape the practices of leading, teaching and learning as they develop in a rich ecology of practices.

Regional profile | Asia-Pacific | Japan

Play is central to nurturing young children in Japanese ECEC settings. Japanese ECEC is rooted in play-oriented programs, as mandated by the government and Article 31 of the United Nations Convention on the Rights of the Child (UNICEF, 1989). Programs place significant emphasis on guiding children to develop fundamental human attributes rather than fixating on academic skills. Early childhood teachers prioritise play to foster holistic development. ECEC settings support children in acquiring essential habits, positive attitudes and healthy minds and bodies through group-oriented play experiences (Bautista et al., 2023).

Japanese children enjoy access to various technology-related activities. However, educators perceive technology as an integral part of play and leverage it to enrich play. Teachers provide age-appropriate technology tools—such as computers, video recorders and digital cameras—to facilitate children's exploration and creativity. By seamlessly integrating technology into play, educators aim to broaden children's perspectives and enhance their communication skills. Japan embodies a dual identity that embraces technological progress while safeguarding cultural heritage. Cultural wisdom is held in high regard and therefore has a key place in educational programs and practices in ECEC.

Japanese parents positively embrace ECEC programs. The values of empathy, culture and technology use child-rearing practices that build on the work of ECEC settings. Parents adjust their expectations as children progress to primary school to align with the standardised test system prevalent in Japanese schools. Japanese ECEC emphasises play, integrates technology thoughtfully and balances modernity with cultural preservation. Through play, children construct knowledge, develop social skills and explore their world within caring and group-oriented communities (Bautista et al., 2023; De Moll & Inaba, 2023).

Reflective questions

How do children's practices influence the emergence and cultivation of leadership?

What role do co-researching with children and respectfully incorporating children's interests into curriculum and planning play in leadership development?

Educators' pedagogical practices (leading, teaching and learning)

ECEC pedagogical practices encompass philosophies of teaching and learning, educational learning frameworks and practices of teaching. Learning frameworks drive the educational programs within them, and 'ongoing investigation, collaboration, and research between adults and children as an everyday praxis (Reggio Children, 2022) ... shift social-political arrangements and

The Complex Site of ECEC

makes it possible for educators to engage in teaching, learning, and leading practices' (Salamon et al., 2024, p. 5).

Region profile | South America | Chile

Chile has proactively prioritised ECEC through targeted public policy initiatives. These policies are designed to address multifaceted aspects of ECEC and elevate its overall quality. Recent policy endeavours within Chile's broader educational system have centred on quality improvement. Educators play a pivotal role in translating these policies into practice and significantly shape the educational experiences of young children across the country (Cárcamo, 2018).

Emerging tensions in the Chilean ECEC system arise from the interplay between the discourses of early childhood teachers and public policies. These tensions are linked to the 'schoolarization' of ECEC and the pursuit of quality. Teachers' perspectives and responses to public policy highlight the multifaceted nature of policy implementation. An analysis of these tensions through the lenses of agency, power dynamics and discourses contributes to a nuanced understanding of professional identity within the field of ECEC (Cárcamo, 2018; Viviani, 2016).

Professional development plays a pivotal role in enhancing the effectiveness of ECEC teachers. Given their substantial influence on children's learning and development, continuous growth and learning are essential. Educators gain new insights, refine their teaching practices through professional development programs and stay abreast of the latest research and methodologies. According to the OECD (2022b), action research, within the framework of a socio-cultural perspective, has emerged as a valuable approach to teacher development. It centres on improving pedagogical interactions in the classroom. By engaging in systematic inquiry, teachers reflect on their practices, identify areas for improvement and implement evidence-based strategies. This dynamic process fosters professional growth, which benefits young children and the quality of their experience in ECEC. Additionally, educators are empowered with knowledge about quality standards (Viviani, 2016).

Reflective questions

How do educators' practices of reflection build their practices of leading?
How does resistance to movements such as 'schoolarization' enable early childhood teachers to develop and enact leadership?

Partnerships with families, communities and societies

Discourses of partnerships with families and communities in ECEC government policy reflect the social-political arrangements of ECEC that enable participation and collaboration of families and the community within ECEC settings.

Regional profile | Eastern Europe | Hungary

Hungary has made some gains in formulating early childhood development policies and supporting families with young children. The availability of ECEC services for children under three years of age—such as nurseries and creches—has modestly increased. This growth is attributed to the implementation of flexible service models, including small-scale nurseries in settlements with fewer children and workplace-based childcare facilities. Despite these positive developments, parental leave entitlements in Hungary are extensive, and this leads to fewer enrolments of children under three in ECEC programs. A prevailing public sentiment persists that day care may not be optimal for children in this age group (OECD, 2022a). Additionally, the lack of awareness-raising campaigns to promote ECEC among families compromises its use.

Despite efforts, disparities persist in providing equitable access to services for all children. The concentration of services in large municipalities poses a challenge, which leaves rural and remote areas under-served. Additionally, private options, though limited, tend to be costly, and this exacerbates inequities. While the number of ECEC facilities has increased, more is needed to meet the demand. Children from more affluent families benefit from less crowded settings, while marginalised groups—such as the Roma community and economically disadvantaged children—often encounter less favourable conditions (Mikuska, 2021). Further, the inclusion of children with special needs remains inadequate, and settings lack specialised educators (Kovács, 2020). Addressing these challenges requires concerted efforts to bridge gaps and ensure that every child has access to high-quality early education and care.

Research on parent–practitioner partnerships still needs to be expanded despite the significant importance of nurturing collaborative relationships between families and ECEC providers. To enhance services, several steps are required (OECD, 2022b). First, gaining insights into the unique needs,

The Complex Site of ECEC

expectations and cultural contexts of families is crucial. This understanding allows educators to tailor their approaches and create meaningful connections with parents. Second, collecting and analysing data related to access and affordability of ECEC services are vital. This information identifies gaps and areas for improvement to ensure equitable opportunities for all families. Lastly, strengthening coordination between government structures, ECEC institutions and community organisations is key. Collaborative efforts can lead to effective policies, resource allocation and support for families (Mikuska, 2021).

Reflective question

How are the practices of leading cultivated and developed through engagement with families, communities and society?

This broad analysis of six systems of ECEC in regions through the lens of the education complex highlights the similarities and differences between jurisdictional policy and practice. These comparisons illuminate the variations in sites where leading and leadership emerges and develops.

How do these educational practices influence leadership cultivation and development?

Practices and the spaces in which they occur do not exist in isolation. They are part of an ecology of practices that exist in the education complex. In the theory of practice architectures, ecologies of practices refer to the interconnected relationship between the practices, the arrangements that enable and constrain practices and the site in which practices occur. The conditions of one practice can become the conditions that make other practices possible or impossible and, at times, necessary for their sustainability. As the term 'ecologies' suggests, practices are similar to living entities. They dynamically change and adapt in response to other practices. Further, the ecological arrangement between practices is individual to the site in which the practices take place. An interdependency of practices takes place within the education complex, which constitutes the range of related and interconnected practices (Kemmis et al., 2014).

Conclusion

Leading and leadership in ECEC around the world are practised in a complex milieu of people, policy and practices often without adequate preparation, systemic support or professional development. A sound grasp of the complex environment where leading is enacted and an understanding of the skills, knowledge and values that characterise effective leadership underpin the planning for the emergence and development of leadership within early childhood organisations. Chapters 5 and 6 explore the conditions and strategies for this emergence and development and identify practical approaches to cultivating leadership that are informed by theory and research.

Reflective questions

Consider the complex environments where you work and lead and the six components of the education complex.

Reflect on the six elements of the education complex according to Gibbs and Press (2023): children's learning and practice; pedagogy; initial teacher education and professional learning; education policy and administration; leadership, research and quality assessment; and partnerships with families and community.

How does leading happen in each of these elements in your organisation, and how is leading shaped by the six elements?

References

Australian Productivity Commission. (2014). *Childcare and Early Childhood Learning*. https://www.pc.gov.au/inquiries/completed/childcare/report

Bautista, A., Yu, J., Lee, K., Sun, J. (2023). Impact of play-based pedagogies in selected Asian contexts: What do we know and how to move forward? In R. Maulana, M. Helms-Lorenz & R. M. Klassen (Eds), *Effective teaching around the world* (pp. 473–488). Springer, Cham. https://doi.org/10.1007/978-3-031-31678-4_21

Brown, B. C. (October 2011). Complexity leadership: An overview and key limitations [Learner paper: Complexity leadership]. *Integral Leadership Review*. http://integralleadershipreview.com/3962-learner-paper-complexity-leadership/

Cárcamo, R. A. (2018). Early childhood education in Chile. In M. Fleer & B. van Oers (Eds), *International handbook of early childhood education* (pp. 825–832). Springer. https://doi.org/10.1007/978-94-024-0927-7_41

Carmody-Bubb, M. (2023). *Cognition and decision making in complex adaptive systems: The human factor in organizational performance*. Springer Nature.

Center for the Study of Child Care Employment, National Institute for Early Education Research & Bellwether Education Partners. (2020). *50-State early educator policy and practice research* [2020 Report]. Early Educator Investment Collaborative. https://earlyedcollaborative.org/grants/research-reports/, https://earlyedcollaborative.org/assets/2020/12/EEIC_Report_50StateEarlyEducatorPolicy_2020.pdf

Cilliers, P. (1999). 'Complexity and postmodernism. Understanding complex systems' Reply to David Spurrett. *South African Journal of Philosophy, 18*(2), 275–278. https://doi.org/10.1080/02580136.1999.10878188

De Moll, F. & Inaba, A. (2023). Transformations of early childhood in Japan: From free play to extended education. In D. Bühler-Niederberger, X. Gu, J. Schwittek & E. Kim (Eds), *The emerald handbook of childhood and youth in Asian societies: Generations between local and global dynamics* (pp. 83–106). Emerald Publishing Limited.

Drucker, P., & Wartzman, R. (2010). *The Drucker lectures: essential lessons on management, society, and economy*. McGraw Hill.

Einarsdottir, J., Purola, A., Johansson, M., Broström, S. & Emilson, A. (2015). Democracy, caring and competence: Values perspectives in ECEC curricula in the Nordic countries. *International Journal of Early Years Education, 23*(1), 97–114. https://doi.org/10.1080/09669760.2014.970521

Gibbs, L., Press, F., & Wong, S. (2019a). Complexity leadership theory: a framework for leading in Australian early childhood education settings. In P. Strehmal, J. Heikka, E. Hujala, J. Rodd, & M. Waniganayake (Eds.), *Leadership in Early Education in Times of Change.* (pp. 173–186). Verlag Barbara Budrich.

Gibbs, L., Press, F., & Wong, S. (2019b). Compliance in a landscape of complexity: Regulation and educational leadership. In L. Gibbs & M. Gasper (Eds.), *Challenging the intersection of policy with pedagogy.* (pp. 159–174) Routledge.

Gibbs, L., & Press, F. (2023). The emergence and cultivation of leadership within early childhood education. In *Handbook on Leadership in Education* (pp. 458–473). Edward Elgar Publishing.

Greve, A. & Hansen, O. H. (2018). Toddlers in Nordic early childhood education and care. In M. Fleer & B. van Oers (Eds), *International handbook of early childhood education* (pp. 907–927). Springer. https://doi.org/10.1007/978-94-024-0927-7_47

Härkönen, U. (2002). The process of creating the pedagogical systems theory for early childhood and preschool education. In M. Waniganayake, M. Veisson, E. Hujala & P. K. Smith (Eds), *Global perspectives in early childhood education: Diversity, challenges, and possibilities* (pp. 47–66). Peter Lang.

Hayes, N., O'Toole, L. & Halpenny, A. M. (2023). *Introducing Bronfenbrenner: A guide for practitioners and students in early years education* (2nd ed.). Routledge.

Hazy, J., & Uhl-Bien, M. (2015). Towards operationalizing complexity leadership: How generative, administrative and community-building leadership practices enact organizational outcomes. *Leadership, 11*(1), 79–104. https://doi.org/10.1177/1742715013511483

Hogan, L. (2019). *RE: Administration for Children and Families (ACF) notice: Improving access to affordable, high quality child care: Request for information (RIN 0970-ZA15)* [Correspondence]. National Association for the Education of Young Children. https://www.naeyc.org/sites/default/files/wysiwyg/user-74/naeyc_comment.acf_rfi_on_child_care.pdf

Izumi-Taylor, S., Ito, Y., Lin, C. H. & Lee, Y. Y. (2014). Pre-service teachers' views of children's and adults' play in Japan, Taiwan, and the USA. *Research in Comparative and International Education*, *9*(2), 213–226. https://doi.org/10.2304/rcie.2014.9.2.213

Jorde Bloom, P. (1991). Child care centers as organizations: A social systems perspective. *Child and Youth Care Forum*, *20*(5), 313–333. https://doi.org/10.1007/BF00757061

Jorde Bloom, P. (2005). *Blueprint for action: achieving center-based change through staff development* (2nd ed.). New Horizons.

Kamerman, S. B. & Gatenio-Gabel, S. (2007). Early childhood education and care in the United States: An overview of the current policy picture. *International Journal of Child Care and Education Policy (Seoul)*, *1*(1), 23–34. https://doi.org/10.1007/2288-6729-1-1-23

Kemmis, S., Edwards-Groves, C., Wilkinson, J., & Hardy, I. (2012). Ecologies of practices. In *Practice, learning and change*. (pp. 33–49). Springer.

Kemmis, S., Wilkinson, J., Edwards-Groves, C., Hardy, I., Grootenboer, P., & Bristol, L. (2014). Praxis, practice and practice architectures. In S. Kemmis, J. Wilkinson, C. Edwards-Groves, I. Hardy, P. Grootenboer, & L. Bristol, *Changing practices, changing education* (pp. 25–41). Springer.

Kovács, K. (2020). Inclusion of intellectually disabled children in early childhood education in Hungary in the light of the law. *International Dialogues on Education*, *7*(2), 70–79. https://doi.org/10.53308/ide.v7i2.3

La Paro, K. M., Thomason, A. C., Lower, J. K., Kintner-Duffy, V. L. & Cassidy, D. J. (2012). Examining the definition and measurement of quality in early childhood education: A review of studies using the ECERS-R from 2003 to 2010. *Early Childhood Research & Practice*, *14*(1), article 4. https://ecrp.illinois.edu/v14n1/laparo.html

Lund, S. (2022). The geographic periphery as architecture for leadership practice with Swedish primary school principals: a peripatetic leading practice. *International Journal of Leadership in Education*, 1–20. https://doi.org/10.1080/13603124.2022.2027526

Marion, R. (2008). Complexity Theory for Organizations and Organizational Leadership. In M. Uhl-Bien & R. Marion (Eds.), *Complexity Leadership Part 1: Conceptual Foundations*. Information Age Publishing, Inc.

Marion, R., & Gonzales, L. (2013). *Leadership in education: Organizational theory for the practitioner*. Waveland Press.

Mikuska, E. (2021). The importance of early childhood education and care for Hungarian ethnic minority groups in Romania, Slovak Republic, and Serbia. In N. J. Yelland, L. Peters, N. Fairchild, M. Tesar & M. S. Pérez (Eds), *The SAGE handbook of global childhood* (pp. 383–396). SAGE Publications.

National Association for the Education of Young Children. (2024). *Interested in Accreditation?* https://www.naeyc.org/accreditation/early-learning/interested

Organisation for Economic Co-operation and Development. (2022a). Early childhood education and care for children under age three in Hungary. In *Reducing the gender employment gap in Hungary* (pp. 80–100). OECD Publishing. https://doi.org/10.1787/c2c32cbb-en

Organisation for Economic Co-operation and Development. (2022b). How do early childhood education systems differ around the world? In *Education at a glance 2022: OECD indicators* (pp. 144–165). OECD Publishing. https://doi.org/10.1787/63190ffa-en

Salamon, A., Gibbs, L. & Cooke, M. (2024). Democratic Practices with and for Our Youngest Citizens: Early Childhood Education, Agency, and the Education Complex in *World Worth Living In (Volume 2)*. Springer.

Schneider, M. & Somers, M. (2006). Organizations as complex adaptive systems: Implications of complexity theory for leadership research. *The Leadership Quarterly, 17*(4), 351–365. https://doi.org/10.1016/j.leaqua.2006.04.006

United Nations Children's Fund. (1989). *Convention on the rights of the child.* https://www.unicef.org/child-rights-convention

Urban, M. (2008). Dealing with uncertainty: challenges and possibilities for the early childhood profession. *European Early Childhood Education Research Journal, 16*(2), 135–152. https://doi.org/10.1080/13502930802141584

Viviani, M. (2016). Creating dialogues: Exploring the 'good early childhood educator' in Chile. *Contemporary Issues in Early Childhood, 17*(1), 92–105. https://doi.org/10.1177/1463949115627906

Waniganayake, M., Cheeseman, S., Fenech, M., Hadley, F., & Shepherd, W. (2023). *Leadership: contexts and complexities in early childhood education* (2nd ed.). Oxford University Press.

Zaslow, M. (2022). Early childhood education and care workforce development: A foundation for process quality [Policy brief no. 54]. In *OECD Education Policy Perspectives*. OECD Publishing. https://doi.org/10.1787/e012efc0-en

PART

III Promise

Promise: the quality of potential excellence to assure someone that one will definitely do something or that something will happen

I think it's that constantly wanting to do things better. We talk about greatness, but there is no such thing as greatness. There is, just for me, that drive to want to evolve and make changes and do things better, and how can we evolve this practice, and what can we look at to make things better for ourselves, to have that passion not die for the children and families within our service, and for the wider community.

—Theresa, emerging leader of 20 years' experience

DOI: 10.4324/9781003277590-8

Organisations Cultivating and Shaping Leadership

5

This chapter

- explains how leading and leadership are shaped by the 'arrangements' of the ECEC organisation
- describes those organisational arrangements of language and culture, material resources, relationships and power
- leads you through a case study of the cultivation of leadership
- provides practice ideas for enabling the development of leadership in ECEC organisations.

Introduction

The preceding chapters of this book have given an understanding of the skills, knowledge and values, according to the three studies, that characterise effective leadership. A perspective on the complex environment where leading is enacted was also described. These concepts underpin the planning for the emergence and development of leadership within early childhood organisations. It is now time to move on to the conditions that shape, enable and constrain leading and leadership as an opportunity for building leadership within early childhood education and care (ECEC) organisations and more broadly within the profession. If leadership is pivotal in shaping ECEC program quality and outcomes, then it is essential to cultivate the leadership knowledge, skills and practices of educators. Such cultivation goes beyond the development of individual leaders. Sustained efforts by

DOI: 10.4324/9781003277590-9

organisations to shape leading and leadership practices in all educators lead to a collective mission for high-quality ECEC and workforce retention (Irvine et al., 2016).

Chapter 5, therefore, positions the cultivation of leadership not only as the responsibility of organisations for people but also as an intentional consequence of organisational arrangements. The term 'arrangements' here refers to the conditions that shape the unfolding practices of leadership. According to Kemmis et al. (2014), there are three kinds of arrangements found within a site that shape practices: the cultural-discursive (evident in culture and language), the material-economic (evident in the physical spaces and material resources) and the social-political arrangements (evident in relationships and power).

This chapter now explores the elements of organisational culture and language, material resources and social-political conditions and arrangements that build leadership from the ground up within ECEC settings as sites of practice. The aim of such an approach is to harness the power of emerging and positional leaders to shape high-quality ECEC settings and to advocate for children, families and the community. This chapter places the leadership development story firmly in the hands of ECEC organisations and disrupts the narrative of the individual, charismatic, all-knowing leader who rises from the team to take charge.

In Chapter 3, the knowledge, skills and values of emerging and positional leaders were described. In Chapter 4, the complex sites of ECEC and organisations were explained. Chapter 5 is a practical application of these concepts and takes a deep dive into how leadership emerges and is shaped by organisational arrangements and the infinite complexity of the environment where ECEC takes place or is managed. This chapter explains how structures and systems that focus upon these elements enable and constrain the cultivation of leadership and develop the practices of leading for all educators, thus expanding the important mission of high-quality ECEC.

In conversation with leaders

In Study 1, positional leaders discussed how they enabled the leadership of educators. Below, Shannon describes her respectful approach that enables program development and guides the values of the ECEC organisation.

> *I see my role as being able to enable everything really, whether it's the children's needs or the staff's needs, and that can be anything. I wrote a reflection after the conference the other day that I shared with the team about how I want them to feel that they've got enough resources and they feel supported and that they can do the projects and the things that they want to do. At the end of the day, you want this to be a place where you want to come, whether you're a child or an educator. In terms of leadership, I don't want to actually say "This is what we're doing" and run the programs. I'm not working with the children, but I want to enable them to be able to do the things that they want to do and just set the values or the underlining values of how we work together.*
>
> —Shannon, Study 1

How leading and leadership are shaped by the 'arrangements' of the ECEC organisation

Arrangements are described through the lens of the theory of practice architectures (Kemmis et al., 2014), which, in this case, sheds light on how social life and education are produced, reproduced and transformed within practices, specifically the practices of leading. According to this theory, practices are composed of sayings, doings and relatings embodied in the elements of knowledge, skills and values (see Chapter 3). These elements are enabled and constrained by specific arrangements present at the site where the practice occurs. Cultural-discursive arrangements include the language, discourses and norms that shape the practice. Material-economic arrangements involve the resources, tools and physical conditions that influence the practice. Social-political arrangements relate to power and solidarity, institutional structures and social relations affecting the practice. These arrangements are described below in the context of ECEC, and the findings that relate to the emergence and cultivation of leadership in Study 1 (Gibbs, 2022) are described.

Cultivating Leadership in Early Childhood Education and Care

How do cultural-discursive arrangements contribute to leadership emergence and development?

Cultural-discursive arrangements encompass the organisational culture and language, such as elements of trust and confidence, compliance with regulation along with innovation, professional knowledge, coaching and mentoring, and the development and implementation of philosophy and vision.

Cultural-discursive arrangements that create the conditions for the emergence and development of leadership on each site comprise cultures of trust, the use of professional knowledge and language, and the development of philosophy and values. All three studies, introduced in the Prologue and described in the Appendix, found that significant cultures of trust existed within all sites of ECEC. Where educators felt trusted by their leaders, their own practices of leadership developed. The practices of leadership went beyond planning for children's learning to making decisions on regulation and compliance. A story of trust, below, demonstrates how trust enabled the confidence and leadership of an educator, Theresa, in Study 1.

A story of trust

Theresa was passionate about the inclusion of children with special needs. She had developed her knowledge of inclusion and wanted to take the program in a different direction. After reflecting on the change with her director, she began to support the team to make those changes. The director made herself available for further consultation but was clear with Theresa that this was her project. Theresa thrived in the knowledge that she was trusted and had the support of her director, and the program changes enabled the inclusion of children who had previously not accessed the preschool. Theresa reflected on this culture of trust:

> We are all able to have leadership in the work that we do. We are all able to have our own ideas, our own personalities, our own interests, our own passions and desires. We are the ones making that happen. I can run that program with the trust of my director to go and lead it.
>
> (Theresa, in Gibbs, 2022, p. 13)

Professional knowledge also plays a large role in decision-making. Professional knowledge of, for example, regulatory compliance and innovative pedagogical

Organisations Cultivating and Shaping Leadership

practice is gained through acquiring qualifications and post-qualification training on regulations provided by an employer. This knowledge is important in leading critical thinking and 'speaking to' regulatory authorities on matters of law and regulation. Frida, an educational leader, shows this capacity to challenge accepted 'norms' through a position informed by knowledge gained through professional learning.

A story of professional knowledge

> *Frida, a recently appointed educational leader, studied the early childhood laws and regulations via training provided by the organisation. The knowledge gained meant her pedagogical decision-making was informed by the law rather than by hearsay. She noted that the knowledge gained through professional development gave her the voice to challenge rumours about new regulations. 'I feel that's more empowering because I can say I've got something to argue with rather than just a flat out, "Well that's ridiculous! That can't be right!"…actually, going and finding out why.'*

(Gibbs et al., 2019a, p. 166)

This professional knowledge that Frida describes also embeds itself in professional language used in settings and organisations. Professional language imbues a sense of pride in the profession and encourages collectivity in leading a vision to achieve high quality.

Other arrangements found in all three research studies include the following:

Inclusive language plays a pivotal role in shaping organisational policies. These policies are designed to foster a sense of responsibility among all stakeholders. The governance and management policy underscores the importance of values and philosophy throughout organisations, creating a culture that respects diversity and promotes inclusivity. Compliance with laws and regulations is seen not as a burden of responsibility for a few but rather as a shared responsibility for all employees, educators, positional leaders and organisational management.

The concepts of 'trust' and 'inclusion' are deeply embedded in the statements of philosophy and vision across ECEC organisations. This language is

Cultivating Leadership in Early Childhood Education and Care

not confined to policy documents but permeates professional conversations, reflecting a commitment to these values in everyday interactions. The philosophies of these organisations explicitly acknowledge trust as a defining factor in relationships with children and families. This recognition underscores the importance of building strong, trusting relationships as a foundation for effective education and care.

From the perspective of emerging leaders, trust is significant in their interactions with children. They recognise and respect children's capabilities, and this trust forms a fundamental principle guiding their practice. Goal setting, a key aspect of leadership, often revolves around fostering trust and respect within the community. By doing so, emerging leaders aim to create an environment where every child feels valued and empowered, promoting a positive learning culture.

The development of vision and philosophy and approaches to vision and philosophy development vary, and all increase emerging and positional leaders' professional knowledge and collective practice:

- Senior leaders guide the establishment, while site leaders refine the language collaboratively.
- Other ECEC settings involve all staff in building the vision and philosophy 'from the ground up'.

How do material-economic arrangements contribute to leadership emergence and development?

Material arrangements contribute to the conditions that allow for the emergence and development of leading and leadership in ECEC. In this framing, organisational material resources include the physical spaces of an ECEC setting, pedagogical resources, professional learning, and the development opportunities and training. These underpin leadership cultivation and growth.

As an example, Louise below discusses professional learning as a material resource that contributes to leadership development. The first experience is a program with a workshop structure, and the second is an immersive study tour. Each experience makes a contribution to the development of leading.

110

A story of leadership cultivation through professional learning

Over the last couple of years, before we amalgamated and just at the point of amalgamation there were modules that were presented around how to identify leadership, how to work as a high performing team and there was…we just called it our VUCA training.

It was rolled out across council, starting with the leadership team.

The presenter was very dynamic and it was really well presented, really accessible with a lot of good messaging, not theoretically and not deeply theoretical, but for people who have not heard about Maslow, they heard about Maslow. For people who, needed skills in moving people forward-that was there too. The modules included topics like getting the best out of your team members, supervising, management poor work performance. Those were some of the big banner headings. But then working through the ways you can work with yourself, recognise your own spot in the whole leadership management area and then understanding how you can get teams onboard, looking at performing teams, low performing teams, high performing teams and what it contributes. The presenter used flip charts, never used a whiteboard and did a lot of the talking ad lib. It was an interesting way of doing the training.

–Louise, Study 1

I was offered the opportunity as a part of my role to do a ten day the study tour in Japan. My agenda was to look at child care, children services and early education as a way to increase the population

I learnt so much about respect, listening, being out of my comfort zone, that I'm quite wise in my older years. But I learned a lot about the sadness that is in Japan around the lack of population and the struggle that is going on to increase the population, for their agendas around improving the numbers of children and of people in Japan.

It was 24/7 experience of being immersed in Japanese community and accompanied by local people with translators and having official meetings with the local government and Council of International Relations.

> *This tour inspired me to talk with our council managers about what I saw and experienced I want to show them what's in Igashena—the three storey indoor play room with the mother's group next door to the family day care, next door to the health clinic in this fantastic multipurpose, multifunctional state of the art building which is next door to the most beautiful library with a café and training rooms.*
>
> *–Louise, Study 1*

As a material arrangement, professional learning for leading clearly takes different forms in different organisations (Gibbs, 2022). For example, an organisation that is going through significant change may allocate resources to supporting emerging and positional leaders to increase agility and confidence and to know how to support educators during periods of change. Other ECEC organisations focus on developing emerging leaders through training in matters of compliance, administration and regulations so they can apply this knowledge in their everyday practices of leading, exercise professionalism and speak to the regulations.

Annette, a leader of professional learning in a large organisation, notes the importance of diversifying approaches to leadership development.

> *I don't believe there is a 'one way' and I think that's why ... because leadership is so complex and in terms of leadership, you can lead with courage, you can actually lead from behind, which I would see probably my role in this team but then when needing to having to step forward and make some of those hard decisions, it's not a free for all, because that's still required.*
>
> *I think it has to be around where that person is at, where that organisation is at because if we just roll out a program as such without acknowledgment of where people are at, where organisation culture is at then our expectations can't be met; and I think some of that is really unpacking the current culture. I think it's having some of those really critical conversations.*
>
> *You're probably more moving into some really strong mentoring programs for professional learning and that could be individual mentoring or group mentoring.*
>
> *– Annette, Study 1*

Organisations Cultivating and Shaping Leadership

The material resources that support the development of leading and leadership go beyond professional development. Across the three organisations within the three studies, common material-economic arrangements influenced leadership emergence and development. These arrangements included themes related to physical space, the allocation of resources and professional learning for leadership (Gibbs, 2022).

Physical spaces played a crucial role in shaping leadership practices across all sites. The design and utilisation of physical spaces were key in cultivating effective leadership practices. These environments, extending beyond play areas, become places for active supervision, where educators participate in coaching, mentoring and pedagogical dialogues. Shared lunchrooms and outdoor spaces were places for the cross-pollination of ideas and informal coaching discussions.

Effective team communication and innovative pedagogical decision-making were facilitated by strategic resource allocation and thoughtful room layout. For example, Shannon, the centre director in Study 1, leveraged localised decision-making to implement site changes and empower teaching initiatives. This dynamic approach enabled a collaborative and effective environment for educators to lead practice.

Furthermore, in Study 1, each organisation's professional learning initiatives underscored distinctive approaches to nurturing leadership capacity. These approaches were shaped by the governance arrangements within each organisation, which in turn influenced their philosophies regarding professional development and the resources they made available.

How do social-political arrangements contribute to leadership emergence and development?

Organisational social-political arrangements contributing to the cultivation of leadership within ECEC settings comprise power, role equality, disruption and creativity, and comprehensive programs of employment induction. Governance structures are included in these arrangements along with structural roles such as educational leader and centre director. Additionally, centre and government policy plus regulation, quality assessment, role and roster descriptions, advocacy, creativity and innovation enable and constrain the cultivation of leading. Across the sites within the three studies, common social-political arrangements influenced leadership emergence and development. These arrangements included themes of role equality, contested role equality and sharing of power (Gibbs, 2022).

In Study 1, the social-political arrangements were exemplified in actions around role equality and the sharing of power. Staff meetings and professional development events exemplified role equality. During these gatherings, meeting agendas often emerged organically, and discussions were led by both emerging leaders and those in positional roles. Notably, students and volunteers actively participated, confidently sharing their passions and interests. Contributions to decisions and strategic direction were welcomed unconditionally, regardless of qualifications or experience. This commitment to role equality fostered an environment of inclusivity and openness.

Hierarchical language was consciously avoided in order to maintain a balanced approach to role equality. Staff members remained vigilant, ensuring that no team member felt disempowered. By acknowledging and addressing potential disparities, the organisation upheld the principles of role equality.

Within this context, an implicit expectation existed that everyone shared responsibility for implementing regulations. Decision-making was localised, allowing for agility and adaptability based on site-specific needs. This collaborative approach not only empowered all team members but also underscored the trust and importance placed in each individual's contribution to the organisation's success.

In conversation with emerging leaders: How do you feel about working here?

There is room at the table for everyone. Like, you've knocked on the door at dinner time, 'Come and eat with us.' The door is always open. No matter who you are, no matter where you've come from, you are welcome here. I think that's something I really connect to.

It all comes back to the idea that there is no right way to do it according to the powers that be. There's nothing that states how the job has to be done, it just states that you must have one (educational leader). So, from that perspective, it gave us the flexibility to look at the former educational leader's strengths versus my strengths and how I could bring other things to the role and do the role a little bit differently.

This is a place where I want to be at this point because it's passionate, it's forward thinking, it's all these things that I love, and it challenges me as well. You don't want to go to a place that it's all the same every day. That's not the place that I want to be.

(Theresa in Gibbs, 2022, p. 16)

How do governance practices influence the development of leadership and management in ECEC organisations?

The governance practices within ECEC organisations play a critical role in shaping leadership and management. The TALIS Starting Strong report (Nilsen et al., 2020) emphasises the significance of critical responsibilities, functions and organisational structures for leaders within ECEC centres. These responsibilities extend to emerging leaders and teams of educators and influence their professional growth, job satisfaction and overall well-being.

However, it is essential to recognise that working conditions, policies, funding practices, regulations, monitoring and quality assessment can vary significantly across different countries. As a result, there is no one-size-fits-all approach to governance. What works effectively in one context may not be suitable for another.

Despite this diversity, effective governance practices create an enabling environment for leadership and management development within ECEC organisations. By fostering transparent decision-making, accountability and collaboration, these practices enhance the quality of ECEC services.

Case study: Leading change-cultivating leadership

When I was employed by the organisation, it was clear that one of my roles was to improve quality. Pedagogical practices were patchy within the organisation, and high staff turnover meant that it was difficult to have a consistency of care and education for the children from babies to six-year-olds. The physical environment reflected an apathy that was apparent in educators' discussions about their practice.

I took time to observe and analyse what was going on. There had been three directors of the setting in just two years, and those staff who had stayed were fatigued by the number of changes and different approaches to decision-making. I could see that educators were not confident to make decisions on their own. It would have been easy to place fault with educators, but there was a lot going on in the organisation that disempowered them.

Once I had my own thoughts together, I gathered the team together for dinner and discussion. Although attendance was compulsory, some staff called in to say they couldn't make it. This was the first of our honest conversations. These conversations expanded into monthly gatherings where we reflected on our culture, our physical space and how we shared roles. Once the team had their voices heard and were part of changes, they began to trust the process. Eventually, everyone came along for the monthly dinners, and these became a highlight for us all. Through this process of reflection and collaboration, changes emerged. Both leaders and educators took responsibility for implementing change. For example, our physical space needed some intensive care. Two educators who were passionate about the outdoor environment took up the challenge to transform the space. They talked with our children and families and asked the team for thoughts. They asked for some resources to make changes. Long story short, we now have a long term plan for a playground renovation and in the meantime, the two staff have created gardens and some beautiful outdoor spaces that we all love and really enhance our programming.

We still have a lot of work to do, but I'm confident we are on the way. I see it in the faces and actions of the team. They are leading every day now in the work they do. The apathy is gone!

–Laney, Study 2

Unpacking the case study through a practice lens

This story could be a 'triumph' and outcome of good leadership, but let us look more deeply at the organisational practices and arrangements that made the changes possible.

The organisational arrangements

- o a commitment to improvement
- o time to reflect
- o existing measures and standards of quality
- o dinner gatherings
- o educator passions
- o philosophy of dispersed leadership.

Shaped the practices of leading educational program and practice, physical change to the environment and revived professionalism and collaboration.

Organisations Cultivating and Shaping Leadership

Over to you: Practical ideas for enabling the development of leading and leadership in ECEC organisations

Chapter 1 argued for changing how we see and develop sustainable leadership. This current section of the book is focused on your organisation and how it enables leading and leadership, provides pathways for leadership and practices sustainably. In this section, you are guided through practical steps to consider how your leadership is developed and how the practices of leading are enabled within your ECEC setting and broader ECEC organisations. This chapter proposes that organisations must do the 'heavy lifting' to make leadership cultivation possible; thus, the chapter maintains that it is not the responsibility of the individual leader to rise, develop charisma and take control. Chapter 6 more thoroughly investigates how professional learning contributes to leadership development.

The why, what and how of developing leading and leadership

First, the 'why': The purpose of leadership in ECEC

In 2008, leadership scholar Amanda Sinclair asked, 'What is all this leadership for?' Sinclair's work on leadership in the provocatively titled *Leadership for the Disillusioned* (2008) challenges the conventional wisdom and myths about leadership that have dominated the leadership discourse. She questions the purpose and the outcomes of leadership that are based on assertiveness, confidence, control and heroism. Sinclair argues that such leadership is often driven by narrow interests, ego and fear and that it fails to address the complex and interconnected challenges of the contemporary world.

These complex and interconnected challenges are ever-present in the sites of ECEC, as emerging and positional leaders respond to complicated policy and funding regimes, evolving theory and ECEC practice, workforce precarity, child and family profiles, complex industrial relations landscapes, human resource management and increasing demands from ongoing crises of pandemics and climate disasters (Alchin et al., 2019; Gibbs et al., 2019a; Quinones et al., 2023).

The question of the purpose of ECEC leadership, therefore, influences the response to this complexity and shapes pathways to and cultivation of leadership.

The drivers for the enactment of leadership are visible through the various lenses of social justice and advocacy, child development, growth of citizens of the future, progress of the profession, development of others and their leadership, workforce sustainability compliance, educational quality and even profit for shareholders. With such a multitude of drivers, the underlying intentions of leadership must be clear to shape the pathways to leadership, to research and to practice leading that avoids a leadership ideology that Sinclair (2008) describes as leading to 'punishing and ultimately unsustainable ways of working and living' (p. 320). Positional leaders have often had inadequate practice of 'leading' (Sinclair, 2008; Waniganayake et al., 2017) and may shape their own leadership to a charismatic, individualistic model unsustainable for organisations and individuals both within and outside the ECEC sector. Understanding the central premise for leadership provides a foundation for further development of research and the practice of leading in ECEC.

The premise of this book is that at the very heart of effective leadership in ECEC is its influence on the quality of ECEC programs and that high-quality ECEC programs have a formidable effect on children's academic, emotional and social outcomes and life trajectories; therefore, effective leadership in early childhood education (ECE) plays a role in the development of civil and economically productive societies. Arguably, the abovementioned additional drivers (e.g., regulatory compliance and profit for shareholders) are fundamental for leadership cultivation and development, as these demand important skills for the role but sit at the periphery. At this stage, you may wish to return to your reflections in Chapter 3 to remind yourself what your leadership is for.

Next the 'what': knowledge, skills and values of emerging and positional leaders

Chapter 3 examined the knowledge, skills and values that make up the disposition of leaders specifically: knowledge is described as forms of understanding embodied in cognitive knowledge, thinking and perceptions that are the foundation of 'sayings'; skills describes the modes of action and capabilities in carrying out practices ('doings'); values describes relating to others and the world ('relatings'; Kemmis et al., 2014). Additionally, it is the development of the practices of leading that are foundational to the emergence and cultivation of leaders. To think on these matters examining and 'finding' leadership, consider the Leadership Observation Tool (see Table 5.1), which is designed to help observe leading practices and leadership behaviours. This practical tool serves as a means for self-reflection, dialogue and discussion. Developed for Study 1, it emerged from an extensive literature review that revealed a gap: no existing tool specifically addressed the observation and identification of emergent effective leadership within

Questions	Could be present in arrangements of	Could be observed in practices (but are not limited to)			
		Siraj-Blatchford and Manni (2007)	Coleman et al. (2016)	Standards	Hazy and Uhl-Bien (2015)
What personal, professional and organisational language and communication enhance the emergence and development of leading and leadership in early childhood education and care (ECEC) sites?	Enabling leadership (as defined by Marion and Gonzales, 2013).	Ensure shared understandings, meanings and goals. Communicate well.	Engaging responsively	Communicate well.	Articulate an idealised future with shared values and aspirations. Ask each person to invest their energy and resources in the organisation. Clarify in-group/out-group boundaries, perhaps by using 'us' versus 'them' language.
What are the networks of professional relationships and communication that boost leading and leadership?	Adaptive leadership (as defined by Marion and Gonzales 2013).	Identify and articulate a collective vision. Communicate well.	Clear vision. Understanding of ECEC.	Communicate well. Commit to ongoing professional development. Encourage critical reflection. Statement of philosophy.	Community-Building. Initiate and perform inclusion rituals like group celebrations. Bring diverse experiences and perspectives together and support differences of opinion. Form small teams and rotate membership often to break up stale thinking.

(*Continued*)

Cultivating Leadership in Early Childhood Education and Care

Table 5.1 (Continued)

Questions	Could be present in arrangements of	Could be observed in practices (but are not limited to)			
		Siraj-Blatchford and Manni (2007)	Coleman et al. (2016)	Standards	Hazy and Uhl-Bien (2015)
What personal, professional and organisational resources enhance the emergence of leading and leadership in ECEC sites?	Administrative leadership (as defined by Marion and Gonzales, 2013).	Builds learning community. Builds team culture.	Motivating staff. Uses business skills strategically.	Effectively documented policies and procedures. Appropriate governance arrangements. Establish and maintain administrative systems.	Make people feel they are part of something valued and significant. Use resource allocation authority to 'kill' dead-end projects or wasteful activities. Establish specific task targets, dependencies and deliverables. Provide resources and space to try new things and new directions. Encourage broad adoption of innovations that have been vetted. Build trust that individuals will have access to shared resources.
What skills, understandings and dispositions underpin the development of leading and leadership?	Cultural-discursive, material-economic, social-political. Enable leadership (as defined by Marion and Gonzales, 2013).	Communicate well. Contextual literacy. Critical reflection. Commitment to ongoing professional development. Builds team culture encourages and builds community partnership. Uses evidence to drive improvement and outcomes.	Contextual literacy. Embracing integrated working. Engaging responsively. Committed to own and others' learning. Motivating and coaching staff.	The induction of educators, coordinators and staff members. Commitment to continuous improvement. Performance of educators, coordinators and staff members is evaluated, and individual development plans are in place.	Encourage openness to surprises to learn / do not punish failure. Provide clear roles, task-specific training and follow up on expected activities.

The tool was developed with reference to Coleman et al. (2016), Hazy and Uhl-Bien (2015), Kemmis et al. (2014), Marion and Gonzales (2013) and Siraj-Blatchford and Manni (2007). (Gibbs et al., 2020).

Organisations Cultivating and Shaping Leadership

ECEC sites. The goal of developing it was to pinpoint the characteristics of effective leadership and leadership emergence (Gibbs et al., 2019b).

The tool aligns with complexity leadership theory (CLT) drawn from the work of Marion and Gonzales (2013) and complexity leadership practices as outlined by Hazy and Uhl-Bien (2015) and Uhl-Bien and Arena (2017). Additionally, it incorporates observable effective leadership practices based on empirical research by Siraj-Blatchford and Manni (2007) and Coleman et al. (2016). Further, it integrates quality measures for leadership and governance.

Focusing on inclusive actions, disruption and dynamic interactions, this tool captures the essence of leadership emergence within the context of CLT. During its development, the practices of leading were cross-checked against known characteristics of effective leadership in ECEC, as outlined by the Australian Children's Education & Care Quality Authority (2017) and Siraj-Blatchford & Manni (2007).

Notably, the field observation tool enables the identification of emerging leadership—defined by practices of effective ECEC leadership—framed within the lens of CLT. Notably, it extends beyond formal leadership roles and encompasses the practices of all educators.

This tool could be useful for reflection for educators and leaders. Understanding what makes effective practice is a good starting point for ECEC professionals as they plan their development.

Now the 'how': The arrangements that enable and cultivate the practices of effective leadership

Research, including the three research studies described in this book, shows that particular arrangements are conducive to the emergence and development of leadership. It is useful to consider how each of these arrangements (described in Table 5.2), framed as cultural-discursive, material-economic and social-political, is visible and enacted in your ECEC organisation or setting. The questions for reflection will help members of the organisation consider where additional efforts can be made to support sustainable leadership practice and transformation within people, teams and organisations.

In conclusion

Organisations play a critical role in shaping leadership. It is not the responsibility of the educator or leader to rise up and take control. This expectation

Cultivating Leadership in Early Childhood Education and Care

Table 5.2 Questions for reflection

Arrangements	Questions for reflection
Cultural-discursive arrangements	How do the staff team use professional language in their everyday conversations and discussions regarding early childhood education and care (ECEC)?
	How is a culture of trust generated within the ECEC organisations?
	How can you collectively develop a vision and a philosophy for the ECEC organisations that enhance the cultivation of leadership?
	How can your philosophy become central to decision-making for children, families and staff at the ECEC organisation?
Material-economic arrangements	Are decisions on how resources are allocated within the ECEC organisations made collaboratively?
	Are resources allocated for education programs and practice so that staff teams do not compete for resources?
	Does the physical ECEC setting have space for mentoring conversations and individual supervision?
	Are resources allocated to professional learning on leadership and the practices of leading?
Social-political arrangements	How can you create a culture of activism, creativity and an environment where different perspectives are valued?
	How can educators and leaders be oriented to the history and traditions of their organisations?
	How can emerging leaders learn about the administrative, adaptive and enabling elements of leadership roles?
	How can emerging leaders learn about the context of their ECEC settings through the lens of the education complex? (See Chapter 4.)
	How is power dispersed throughout the ECEC organisation or setting?

leads to unsustainable leadership and perpetuates the myth of heroic leadership.

In this chapter, the lens of the theory of practice architectures has promoted an understanding of the contributions made by cultural-discursive, material-economic and social-political arrangements to the emergence and cultivation of leading and leadership. Applying these theoretical frameworks

Organisations Cultivating and Shaping Leadership

in practice means fostering a culture of trust, leveraging professional knowledge and language, and collaboratively developing visions and philosophies (as highlighted by Rönnerman et al., 2017). Trust can be challenging in a complex culture of compliance, but personal, professional responsibility and organisational communication knowledge empower emerging and positional leaders to act confidently. Philosophy is a vital reference point, especially when emerging and positional leaders intentionally incorporate philosophical language into everyday conversations.

Taking physical spaces and resource allocation into consideration is essential for supporting effective leadership practices. Designated areas separate from children provide educators with useful spaces for pedagogical discussions. Innovative physical environments and shared spaces inspire and promote high-quality practices. Emerging and positional leaders benefit from diverse and generous approaches to professional learning. Understanding the complexity of ECEC environments is essential for building individual and collective capacities on ECEC sites (O'Neill & Brinkerhoff, 2018). Fostering equality empowers emerging leaders to speak confidently, innovate and drive positive changes in educational practice.

Broadening understandings of how leading and leadership are cultivated by the practices and arrangements of organisations creates the opportunity to expand the practice of leading and therefore increase the quality of the ECEC community.

Final questions for reflection

Much of this chapter has been a reflection on practices and arrangements. Final questions for you are to consider decentralising leadership and creating enabling arrangements for the development of the practices of leading.

Where will efforts within your organisation be made to decentralise and develop leading and leadership?

How will the cultural-discursive (evident in culture and language), the material-economic (evident in the physical spaces and material resources) and the social-political arrangements (evident in relationships and power) in your ECEC organisation shape and enable the practices of leading and leadership?

References

Alchin, I., Arthur, L. & Woodrow, C. (2019). Evidencing leadership and management challenges in early childhood in Australia. *Australasian Journal of Early Childhood, 44*(3), 285–297. https://doi.org/10.1177/1836939119855563

Australian Children's Education and Care Quality Authority. (2017). Leadership and management in education and care services. An analysis of Quality Area 7 of the National Quality Standard. *Occasional Paper 5*. https://www.acecqa.gov.au/acecqas-occasional-paper-5-quality-area-7

Coleman, A., Sharp, C. & Handscomb, G. (2016). Leading highly performing children's centres: Supporting development of the 'accidental leaders'. *Educational Management Administration & Leadership, 44*(5), 775–793. https://doi.org/10.1177/1741143215574506

Gibbs, L. (2022). Leadership emergence and development: Organizations shaping leading in early childhood education. *Educational Management Administration & Leadership, 50*(4), 672–693. https://doi.org/10.1177/1741143220940324

Gibbs, L., Press, F., & Wong, S. (2019a). Compliance in a landscape of complexity: Regulation and educational leadership. In L. Gibbs & M. Gasper (Eds.), *Challenging the intersection of policy with pedagogy*. (pp. 159–174) Routledge.

Gibbs, L., Press, F., & Wong, S. (2019b). Complexity leadership theory: a framework for leading in Australian early childhood education settings. In P. Strehmal, J. Heikka, E. Hujala, J. Rodd, & M. Waniganayake (Eds.), *Leadership in Early Education in Times of Change*. (pp. 173–186). Verlag Barbara Budrich.

Gibbs, L., Press, F., Wong, S. & Cumming, T. (2020). Innovative methods for researching leadership emergence. *The Qualitative Report, 25*(8), 2026–2043. https://nsuworks.nova.edu/tqr/vol25/iss8/2/

Hazy, J., & Uhl-Bien, M. (2015). Towards operationalizing complexity leadership: How generative, administrative and community-building leadership practices enact organizational outcomes. *Leadership, 11*(1), 79–104. https://doi.org/10.1177/1742715013511483

Irvine, S., Sumsion, J., Lunn, J., & Thorpe, K. (2016). One in five early childhood educators plan to leave the profession. *The Conversation*. https://eprints.qut.edu.au/102723/

Kemmis, S., Wilkinson, J., Edwards-Groves, C., Hardy, I., Grootenboer, P. & Bristol, L. (2014). Praxis, practice and practice architectures. In S. Kemmis, J. Wilkinson, C. Edwards-Groves, I. Hardy, P. Grootenboer & L. Bristol (Eds), *Changing practices, changing education* (pp. 25–41). Springer.

Marion, R., & Gonzales, L. (2013). *Leadership in education: Organizational theory for the practitioner*. Waveland Press.

Nilsen, T., Slot, P., Cigler, H. & Chen, M. (2020). Measuring process quality in early childhood education and care through situational judgement questions: Findings from TALIS starting strong 2018 field trial. *OECD Education Working Paper* (No. 217). OECD Publishing. https://doi.org/10.1787/19939019

O'Neill, C. & Brinkerhoff, M. (2018). *Five elements of collective leadership for early childhood professionals*. Redleaf Press.

Quinones, G., Berger, E. & Barnes, M. (2023). Promoting care for the wellbeing of early childhood professionals in Australia. *Australasian Journal of Early Childhood, 48*(4), 307–318. https://doi.org/10.1177/18369391231202837

Rönnerman, K., Grootenboer, P. & Edwards-Groves, C. (2017). The practice architectures of middle leading in early childhood education. *International Journal of Child Care and Education Policy, 11*, article 8. https://doi.org/10.1186/s40723-017-0032-z

Sinclair, A. (2008). *Leadership for the disillusioned: Moving beyond myths and heroes to leading that liberates*. Allen & Unwin.

Siraj-Blatchford, I. & Manni, L. (2007). *Effective leadership in the early years sector: The ELEYS study*. Institute of Education, University of London.

Uhl-Bien, M. & Arena, M. (2017). Complexity leadership: Enabling people and organizations for adaptability. *Organizational Dynamics, 46*(1), 9–20. https://doi.org/10.1016/j.orgdyn.2016.12.001

Waniganayake, M., Cheeseman, S., Fenech, M., Hadley, F. & Shepherd, W. (2017). *Leadership: Contexts and complexities in early childhood education* (2nd ed.). Oxford University Press.

Learning for Leading

This chapter explores

- professional learning and the emerging and positional ECEC leader: the state of play
- the leader of the future
- considerations for professional learning
- professional learning for leading
- diverse approaches to professional learning: case studies.

Introduction

Professional learning is a material arrangement within an organisation that enables the emergence and development of leadership in early childhood education and care (ECEC). Material arrangements were explored, in some depth, in Chapters 4 and 5. However, professional learning has an important role in educator and leader development and is therefore worthy of a unique chapter focus. This is because professional learning enhances the opportunity for emerging and positional leaders to develop and transform their practices of leading. This chapter delves into the many aspects of professional learning and examines how to equip leaders with the knowledge, skills and reflective capacity crucial for navigating the complexities of the contemporary ECEC landscape. By fostering a culture of continuous learning, ECEC

DOI: 10.4324/9781003277590-10

organisations have the potential to respond to the evolving context and aspiration for high-quality settings through effective leadership.

Through an exploration of professional learning practices and illuminating stories, this chapter highlights the intrinsic link between comprehensive, innovative professional learning and the cultivation and development of effective leadership. This chapter underscores the significant role that professional learning plays in cultivating and sustaining effective leadership. The ECEC field and profession are continually evolving with new theories, methodologies, policy and regulatory frameworks and new ways of managing people and resources. Ongoing professional learning is therefore a cornerstone of successful leadership cultivation.

A story about professional learning

> *From my first day as a director, I was looking for professional learning. I wanted to make a difference, and I knew a leadership role would be the place to do it, but I was completely unprepared. For the first year, I floundered. A few short courses were helpful, but who really wants to know if their leadership style is a 'peacock' or a 'tiger' when there are families in crisis, staff who need support and compliance to tick off. Then I found my 'people', fellow directors who were also looking for more. We met each fortnight to work through common problems and to critically reflect on our leadership. We coached and mentored each other.*
>
> –Laney, Study 2

> *We overcame our lack of confidence and knowledge together and we grew as leaders. That was the best professional learning I ever had, but I wish I had known more when I started. My development wouldn't have been so painful!*
>
> –Laney, Study 2

Cultivating Leadership in Early Childhood Education and Care

Professional learning and the emerging and positional ECEC leader: The state of play

The lack of structured preparation of ECEC leaders was identified in 1993 by Kagan and Bowen (Ebbeck & Waniganayake, 2003). In 2003, Ebbeck and Waniganayake cited institutional bias, a lack of recognition, poor training, personal attributes of leaders and ambivalence towards power as obstacles to leadership development. Ebbeck and Waniganayake argued that '[h] aving acknowledged these barriers to leadership growth, it is now imperative we move the agenda to new grounds' (Ebbeck & Waniganayake, 2003, p. 28). The lack of movement on leadership development, however, persisted into the next decade within Australia and New Zealand. In Australia, a 2011 Productivity Commission was tasked with a review of the ECEC workforce, which investigated workforce requirements in the context of a growing sector and policy reform. This review identified the lack of professional development for leadership and governance to enhance quality within ECEC settings and build the capability of the workforce (Productivity Commission, 2011). More recently, Waniganayake et al. (2023) and the Australian Children's Education & Care Quality Authority (2020) echoed similar concerns and noted the lack of progress on ECEC leader development despite the requirement for strong governance and educational leadership mandated by Australian policy (Australian Children's Education & Care Quality Authority, 2023).

Preparation for early childhood leadership has been a priority in New Zealand. Funding for professional learning for leadership is, however, diminishing. Despite the drop in funding, there remains a commitment to research-informed professional development to maintain the link between pedagogical quality and leadership implemented within ECEC settings (Denee, 2018). The 'symbiotic' relationship endows head teachers and supervisors with the responsibility to nurture high-quality pedagogical practice and to foster a culture of distributed leadership. Similar to many countries around the world, New Zealand lacks structural preparation for leadership. There is, however, a leadership strategy for ECEC that outlines a vision, principles and capabilities for effective educational leadership in the sector (Education Council, 2018). Developed by the Teaching Council of Aotearoa New Zealand—the Code of Professional Responsibility and the Standards for the Teaching Profession—and based on the values of Te Tiriti o

Waitangi, the strategy supports the development of teachers as leaders. The strategy comprises nine core capabilities or spheres of influence:

- building and sustaining high-trust relationships
- ensuring culturally responsive practice and understanding of Aotearoa New Zealand's cultural heritage
- building and sustaining collective leadership and professional community
- strategically thinking and planning
- evaluating practices in relation to outcomes
- adept management of resources to achieve vision and goals
- attending to their own learning as leaders and their own well-being
- embodying the organisation's values and showing moral purpose, optimism, agency and resilience
- contributing to the development and well-being of education beyond their organisation.

Implementation of the strategy is supported by resources but engagement with professional learning is not mandated in policy or law (Denee, 2018).

Across the US, Greece and Estonia, the intricacies of relational pedagogical leadership are a focus for professional development (OECD, 2019). Relational pedagogical leadership is considered a tool for empowering communities of learners—children, families and educators—where shared decision-making engenders collaborative curriculum development and planning.

Developing leadership and the practices of leading

ECEC leadership researchers commonly focus on the development of the formal leader but also acknowledge the importance of developing the leadership capacity of teachers and educators (Waniganayake et al., 2023). While there is broad agreement on the importance of professional development for ECEC leadership, suitable approaches for both emerging and positional leaders are not commonly available (Rodd, 2012; Waniganayake & Stipanovic, 2016). A formal leadership qualification has not commonly been required under ECEC regulation to lead governance, but changes are afoot in Scandinavian countries and the UK.

In Scandinavia, the role of the pedagogical or educational leader focuses on the quality and content of the curriculum, the learning environment and the professional development of the teaching staff. A complex landscape comprises the increasing diversity of families, new demands of technology and the need to balance expectations of collaborators in other fields of education. The recognition of this complexity has led to regional programs to develop the skills and knowledge of pedagogical leaders and principals in the early years. Methods for development include self-evaluation, peer feedback, mentoring, coaching, action research and professional learning communities (Greve & Hansen, 2018).

Likewise, leadership in ECEC in the UK is becoming increasingly complex. The enactment of leadership must meet the expectations and standards of Ofsted (Office for Standards in Education, Children's Services and Skills), the regulatory body for education and care in the UK (Department for Education, 2024). A National Professional Qualification for Early Years Leadership (NPQEYL), a qualification for leaders who manage early years (ECEC) settings, covers essential skills and knowledge related to leading an early years provision. Participants develop expertise in evidence-informed practices such as establishing and sustaining the strategic direction of the setting, creating an evidence-based teaching culture, planning and delivering care and a high-quality curriculum to support child development, implementing effective communication, language and literacy approaches, and supporting children with additional and special educational needs. Many managers, head teachers and leaders of school-based nurseries have engaged with the funded program provided by universities and training providers.

In other countries (Australia, New Zealand and the US), postgraduate, non-accredited training for leadership regularly takes place within individual organisations. Training employs a range of strategies for leadership development, some of which have more or less successful approaches. For example, a blended action professional leadership development course with a combination of 'face-to-face' and information and communication technology learning was analysed in 2009 (Thornton, 2010). The case study of two action learning groups made up of six ECEC leaders each used interviews, emails, online reflective journals, forum entries and chat sessions to collect data on the efficacy of this professional development course. Findings indicated that the leaders had increased self-awareness and increased confidence in decision-making and delegation. However, this study was mostly based on self-reporting rather than objective measures of effectiveness.

This investigation into leadership development programs by Thornton in 2010 was prompted by signals from the New Zealand Ministry of Education that this area would be a future funding priority. Thornton's exploration involved an analysis of the literature on effective programs, an in-depth review of UK leadership programs and a consideration of how these would work in the New Zealand context (Thornton, 2010). The measure of effectiveness was based on leaders' personal perceptions and improved confidence along with subjective judgements on job performance. There were no explicit measures of service quality improvement. Thornton concluded that effective programs were delivered with broad-ranging strategies that included blended learning (both online and face-to-face delivery), work-based reflection and problem solving, journaling, dialoguing with other leaders, mentoring and coaching and exercises to create greater self-awareness.

Two small research projects investigated the method of reflective inquiry to build leadership capacity. The first project involved two case studies that analysed how oral inquiry was used to support leadership development by strengthening the skills and dispositions of educators to critically reflect upon, explore and negotiate the complex dilemmas in daily practice (Nicholson & Kroll, 2015). The second study was a qualitative research project conducted in the UK with three ECEC leaders over a three-month period using purposeful sampling (Layen, 2015). This phenomenological inquiry analysed leader reflections on autobiographical stories and their effect on leadership effectiveness due to increased self-awareness and self-concept. Layen concluded that autobiographical critical reflection had a constructive effect on participants' views of themselves as leaders and might be another approach to developing leaders. Neither of these studies, however, drew conclusions on how development methods or programs influenced leadership effectiveness.

In a further study of leadership development in the US, the Taking Charge of Change (TCC) program (Talan et al., 2014) measured individual and service effectiveness following participation in a 10-month leadership development program. The strategies employed in the program included skill-building residential schools, written reflections, program improvement plans, mentor support and access to a professional learning community (Talan et al., 2014). This study examined 502 participants across 20 cohorts of TCC participants. Archived data from several measures were also used. These data included a Training Needs Assessment Survey (TNAS), the Program Administration Scale (PAS) (Talan & Bloom, 2004) and the Early Childhood Work Environment Survey (ECWES) (Jorde Bloom, 2016). An online survey of TCC alumni gathered information about their current job status, career

Cultivating Leadership in Early Childhood Education and Care

decisions, continuing professional development, commitment to the ECEC profession and professional achievements. The findings revealed evidence of individual growth and organisational improvement in addition to positive program outcomes relating to accreditation status and participation in Illinois' quality rating system (McCormick Center for Early Childhood Leadership, 2014; Talan et al., 2014). Bloom and Bella (2005) interviewed a subset of 182 TCC participants and found that (i) 86% continued to work in the ECEC profession, (ii) 65% of those continued with the same organisation and (iii) 97% of the directors saw themselves continuing in the profession for five or more years. In addition to improved leadership effectiveness then, the program contributed to a more stable and educated workforce.

In a study, Bøe et al. (2023) investigated how the case method promoted ECEC leadership learning and coping with stress. The exploratory qualitative investigation with 57 ECEC centre directors in Norway found that the case method offered productive learning opportunities for coping with work stress. This study is helpful in illuminating innovative approaches in professional learning that lead to sustainable leadership.

The OECD Teaching and Learning International Survey (TALIS) (2019) investigated the experiences of teachers and early childhood leaders across 48 countries and economies and found that 'lifelong learning' was a critical component of leadership development for staying abreast of evolving educational practices and research. Leaders who engaged in ongoing learning contributed significantly to the growth and improvement of their organisations.

Preparing leaders: What does the leader of the future look like?

Professional development is clearly a key component of the leadership development story, but in planning that professional development, we need to consider the leader of the future, not merely the needs of the leader in the 'here and now'.

The leader of the future

In the study of leadership within a large Australian not-for-profit ECEC organisation (see Study 3), 1500 participants pondered the question of what

Learning for Leading

a leader of the future 'looked like'. The mixed methods study considered the findings of a questionnaire, focus groups, reflective writing and interviews (see Study 3 in the Appendix). Leaders of the future were envisioned.

Early childhood leaders of the future: Who are they and what do they look like?

Leaders reflect the communities in which they work. ECEC positional leaders hold qualifications supplemented with formal qualifications or training and professional development in leadership, management and administration. Additional training and qualifications ideally comprise trauma-informed practice, educator and child well-being, infant and toddler mental health, interdisciplinary knowledge to promote integrated models with allied health professionals and family support workers, and knowledge of information technology.

All leaders in ECEC organisations are skilled in coaching and mentoring. They have sophisticated and consistent approaches to performance development, performance management and collective approaches to systems change. The skill of critical reflection is integral to leadership practice and for use in organisational development. Effective use of time is also an important skill, along with thoughtful prioritisation and focusing efforts where the most can be achieved. Leader qualities include persistence, resilience and the capacity to navigate complex systems. Leaders are enthusiastic about rich experiences as opposed to following a 'standard' career trajectory.

They respond well to a trusting environment that promotes autonomy. Positional leaders must hold ECEC qualifications at a minimum. Non-ECEC positional leaders in ECEC organisations must receive professional development orienting them to the ECEC environment. This creates the opportunity to share ECEC leadership language and to hold a common narrative on high-quality ECEC.

Additional skills and knowledge encompass crisis and complaints management, resilience, innovative approaches to dealing with staffing models and issues, politics, government policy, use of resources, family violence and role management and accountability.

In this research, mentoring, induction and orientation were identified as foundational supports for the leader of the future along with comprehensive training on governance. Spaces for sharing knowledge, either online or physical, create new knowledge and innovative solutions to challenges.

This description provides somewhat of a blueprint for planning professional learning for emerging and positional leaders. There are, however, important considerations and guiding principles prior to planning for professional learning. If organisations are committed to the development of the practices of leading within ECEC, these considerations will inform the strategies and approaches.

Considerations for professional learning

Before creating professional learning for leading, the pedagogy of adult learning, also known as andragogy, must be thoughtfully considered. Understanding the unique characteristics and needs of adult learners is key to effective professional learning. Self-perception, lived experience, motivation and time are among those considerations (Knowles et al., 2014).

Self-perception: Adults perceive themselves as self-directed individuals who want control and responsibility for their own learning. Learning activities should acknowledge and facilitate this intrinsic motivation and allow adults to take an active role in their educational journey.

Experience: Adults bring a range of experiences to any learning environment. Recognising and incorporating these experiences into professional learning foster a rich context for learning. Case-based or scenario learning provides the opportunity to integrate experiences and build new understandings. For example, Bøe et al. (2023), in an examination of 57 ECEC directors' evaluations from the National Leadership Program in Norway, found that the case method offered 'promising learning opportunities for how to cope with work stress through four key themes—social comparison and sharing experiences from real-life cases, group discussions for problem solving, and a learning community for social support and linking practical (coping) tools' (p. 185).

Readiness to learn: People are motivated to learn when they can apply new knowledge to their practice and professional roles. Learning activities that are designed to address real practice challenges align with adult learners' readiness to learn.

Orientation to learning: Adults are purposeful in their approach to learning. Strategies that allow adults to understand the practical outcomes of their efforts and how they connect to their goals are more likely to be effective.

Motivation: Adults are motivated by internal factors such as a desire for personal growth, career advancement or increased competence. Recognising these intrinsic motivators and aligning educational activities with them enhance the engagement and commitment of adult learners.

Need to know: Before committing to the learning process, adults need to understand why they need to learn something. Providing clear objectives and demonstrating the practical application of knowledge help adults see the relevance and importance of the learning content.

How adults learn: Adult learners have diverse learning styles and preferences. Providing a variety of instructional methods, such as visual aids, hands-on activities and group discussions, accommodates these preferences and enhances the learning experience.

Time: Adults are more likely to engage in learning activities that respect their time constraints and are flexible. Offering self-paced learning that allows for flexible scheduling and recognising the demands of adult life contributes to a positive learning environment (Knowles et al., 2014).

These unique characteristics, when considered with the principles and strategies for adult learning described in the following section, provide a framework for professional learning for leading that creates a rich, effective and enjoyable environment for learning and an increased potential for leadership emergence.

Principles for learning

According to Adriano and Rosa (2023), particular principles that comprise high-quality adult learning are briefly discussed below in the context of ECEC. These are a commitment to lifelong learning, personalised plans, reflective practice, practice relevance, collaboration and networking, alignment with organisational goals, integration of technology, feedback and evaluation, ethical considerations, resource management and mentoring and coaching.

Cultivating Leadership in Early Childhood Education and Care

Figure 6.1 Framework for professional learning for leading.

Commitment to lifelong learning: Professional learning is an ongoing proposition. A commitment to lifelong learning enables an understanding of evolving trends, research and best practices in the field of ECEC leadership.

Personalised plans: Emerging and positional leaders will be most committed to learning when learning is shaped to their personal needs that correspond with their interests, passions and organisational needs (see Figure 6.1). The following expression of personal interests by Bridget (a positional leader in Study 1) demonstrates the importance of asking emerging leaders about their interests and passions to inform professional learning.

> *I'm really interested in mental health in young children and I've done some interesting professional development in the past with people who have worked with young babies and looking at mental health.*
>
> *There's lots of things I'm interested in. I'd like to spend some actual immersive time in a Reggio Emilia based service because I have never worked in one before. I have done projects at uni on it and in one of my placements I did some emerging curriculum project work but I think it's very different when you've got the luxury as a student completing emergent curriculum and then doing that on the ground working every day. I think that's hard to see it come full circle. So those are some interest areas for me.*
>
> *I'm also really interested in the Indigenous perspectives in early childhood and so because I'm new to the area I haven't got in contact really with local groups yet and I think that that was potentially*

Learning for Leading

> *... some of those things that I've been interested in, I was really keeping my head above water last year, really just trying to wrap my head around the whole idea of leading this group of educators. Most of them had been here since the start of the service, so to them they felt like they'd been here quite a long time. For me, one and a bit years isn't a long time, but it was one and a bit more years longer than I had. So, they were leading me in certain areas too. So, it was kind of this interweaving of leadership and developing my strengths.*
>
> *—Bridget, Study 1*

Bridget went on to say that an in-depth ECEC curriculum knowledge development was integral to her confidence in leading. This story shows the importance of holding rich, in-depth conversations with emerging and positional leaders about their interests and self-perceived needs rather than imposing a program of development that focuses only on leadership skills.

Reflective practice: Reflective practice is a core component of professional learning and involves reflecting on and analysing practice and then shaping practices in light of new self-knowledge.

Practice relevance: Professional learning activities that relate to practice offer the opportunity to apply new skills and knowledge in the workplace. This experience, combined with reflective practice, creates deep learning.

Collaboration and networking: These foster a culture of collaboration and networking within professional communities. Engaging with peers, mentors and experts to share insights, experiences and resources can enrich everyone's professional development.

Alignment with organisational goals: Professional development initiatives aligned with the strategic goals and vision of the organisation ensure that individual growth contributes to the collective success of the ECEC organisation. The following story from Ros (Study 1) demonstrates an approach that aligns with organisational and individual growth for the development of leaders. Ros is philosophical about individual commitment to the opportunity but notes that there are benefits regardless of whether participants complete the program.

> *We have an internal leadership and mentoring program. We target people who we think have got the capacity and have shown some potential. You have this influx of interest and the first criteria and level, Stage 1, is regulations, national law and quality Some people drop out at Stage 1.*
>
> *The next stage is moving onto the pedagogy of "What does this mean to be a leader? What's the expectations?" Again there's some drop out "Oh, it's not what I thought it was going to be, to be a leader".*
>
> *Some of our best managers have been through that program internally.*
>
> *But we've got to accept that not everybody that starts 'here' is going to get to 'here'. Then there's no guarantee that you're going to be a centre director or a manager of program. It's still a merit based process, but you should have been equipped much better perhaps than others to achieve those positions.*
>
> –Ros, Study 1

Integration of technology: Technology is a tool for professional development if leveraged within online courses, webinars and digital resources to access relevant information, connect with professionals globally and stay abreast of advancements in the field.

Ethical considerations: Incorporating ethical considerations into professional development emphasises the importance of integrity, respect and cultural competence of adult learners.

Resource Management: Efficiently managing time and financial resources maximises learning opportunities without compromising other professional responsibilities.

Mentorship and coaching: Mentoring and coaching relationships facilitate professional development. Learning from experienced colleagues can provide valuable insights and guidance, and it creates an opportunity for knowledge exchange at all levels.

Learning for Leading

A framework for professional learning for leading

However, professional learning for effective leadership development is more than a didactic program for the fulfilment of organisational goals. As noted above, the principles and approaches to development must be learner-centric, be clear on the reason for the learning and be holistic in nature. There are many routes to the development of the practices of leading, and these include not only important sector knowledge but also the professional passions and interests of emerging and positional leaders. A suggested framework for professional learning for leading (see Figure 6.1) considers those needs of the ECEC organisation and, more broadly, the development of the profession, the need for individual development and personal passions and interests.

Organisational and individual needs

Often co-located, these needs may include educational programs and practice, regulation and compliance, and advocacy and child development. Importantly, engaging emerging and positional leaders in learning about these matters is essential to prepare and develop effective leadership. Practice knowledge is essential (Gibbs, 2022).

Evolving educational practices: The field of ECEC is constantly evolving, driven by new research, changing societal needs and technological advances. Professionals must stay updated on the latest best practices and evidence-based methods to provide high-quality education. Continuous professional learning equips leaders with the knowledge and tools to adapt to these changes effectively.

Meeting diverse needs: ECEC serves a diverse population of children with varying abilities and backgrounds. Leaders must have a deep understanding of individualised planning, inclusive practices and cultural competency to meet the unique needs of each child. Professional learning helps leaders acquire these skills.

Regulatory requirements: ECEC is subject to rigorous regulations and standards to ensure the safety and well-being of children. Leaders must be well versed in compliance with these standards, and professional learning is essential for staying current with ever-changing requirements (Gibbs et al., 2019).

Effective pedagogical leadership: Leaders in ECEC need strong pedagogical skills to support their teachers and staff in delivering high-quality instruction. Professional learning enables leaders to develop coaching and mentoring abilities that help educators continually improve their practices.

Advocacy and policy influence: Early childhood leaders play a critical role in advocating for the field and influencing policy decisions at local, state and national levels. Professional learning equips them with the knowledge and skills to advocate effectively and shape policies that benefit young children (Nicholson et al., 2018).

Child development: Leadership in ECEC extends to holding knowledge of social-emotional development, health and well-being. Professional learning helps leaders understand the holistic needs of young children and develop comprehensive programs that support their growth.

Learning shaped to individual and organisational needs equips leaders with the knowledge, skills and competencies required to provide high-quality education, meet the diverse needs of children and navigate the ever-changing landscape of ECEC, ultimately ensuring the best outcomes for young children and their families.

Passions and interests

Research by Fonsén and Soukainen (2020) highlights the importance of professional status and qualifications for sustainable leadership that demands high-quality pedagogy. Leaders and educators also stay in place when they are motivated and inspired in their work and when the work aligns with their values (Fonsén and Soukainen, 2020). Engaging in professional learning that is seemingly unrelated can have a deep effect on leadership. For example, Leora talks about her learning to support relationship building:

> *Becoming a yoga teacher or doing that training and learning more about that made me a better leader. It gave me skills and things about myself that I was able to then implement when I worked alongside other people. I also did a neuroscience to brain health course. That gave me that additional kind skill set or background information. It all comes down to relating to people, right?*
>
> *–Leora, Study 2*

Diverse experiences of professional learning for leading: Three case studies

Research on professional learning for emerging and positional leaders (Gibbs, 2020; Gibbs, 2022) illuminates stories and case studies with successful and creative strategies and approaches. Three case studies, in each of the components of the framework in the above section, 'A framework for professional learning for leading' (organisational needs, individual needs, and passions and interests), are described and examined below in the context of considerations and principles of effective professional learning. These case studies provide examples and highlight the diversity of approaches to professional learning and the principles that pertain to those approaches.

Case study 1: Change management

Framework focus: **Organisational needs**

> *The best professional development training I've been through recently would be the change management. The theory and the process of change management and the neuroscience about it, and the different approaches, that was really insightful. I'm also a big listener to podcasts. A lot of my leadership and my skills have come directly from Brene Brown, Simon Sinek and Adam Grant. Listen to the podcast and they're not talking about anything to do with early childhood. But they talk about humanity. And we work in a human role. So, a lot of what they talk about and practice are brought into the role.*
>
> –Belinda, Study 2

Principles of professional learning: experience, motivation to learn, individualised

Cultivating Leadership in Early Childhood Education and Care

Case study 2: Leadership development

Framework focus: **Individual needs**

We started with the Early Childhood Australia Leadership Capability Framework. Participants work on the capability framework first. It's usually a year and a half in total. The capability framework happens very quickly, and then the remainder of it is where they do a leadership research project where they do leadership in practice. So, they come [and] develop a project that is aligned with the service quality improvement plan. They incorporate theoretical perspectives, their experience, and what their future learning is that they want to do about being a leader, and over time, develop that, and then present what they learnt.

And the biggest growth that we find, in that I try and work with them, is the reflection that they do on themselves as a leader. And what do they learn around that? And then how does that influence their leadership? How they work with other people how they're trying to get people to do whatever it is that their vision is that they're trying to.

In this instance, the educational leader really wanted to understand how to encourage people to be more reflective and do more meaningful documentation.

I think her project brought tears to our eyes this year because she realised that she would tell people what to do, and she'd do an induction, and she was taking people through what the process was. And a few mentoring sessions with me and a few questions later, she ended up realising that she had to find out where each person was at and what they already had to be able to take them to the next step, and I think her statistic was amazing. In the one room, she had 16% engagement with the documentation, and when she presented last week, she had 100% meaningful documentation based on the changes that she implemented.

–Leora, Study 2

Principles of professional learning: practice development, individualised learning

Learning for Leading

> ## Case study 3: Advocacy
>
> Framework focus: **Passions and interests**
>
> *Everybody had this sort of own-advocacy role, and what it was- it was sort of like their own passion project. And what I really liked about that were the moments where we got together to teach each other about those advocacy roles. For me, it was that children's rights. And we would do- start development evenings where we would share information about our roles to try to help other educators understand why they should be working on these sorts of things in their space. It was- things it could be about, you know, physical health, it was about well-being, it was about anything that an educator felt was a strength or an interest. I really liked that because it helped other people explore their own leadership roles. And it meant that we looked at each other as an expert in something and it sort of helped create an environment of respect around knowledge and individual knowledge.*
>
> —Loretta, Study 2
>
> **Principles of professional learning**: motivation to learn, experience

Conclusion

This chapter has established that professional learning is a pivotal arrangement that fosters leadership emergence and evolution. The preceding chapters have laid the groundwork, delving into the organisational arrangements that shape leadership practices. Yet the distinctive focus on professional learning in this chapter illuminates its transformative power for both emerging and positional leaders.

The cultivation of a learning culture within ECEC organisations is instrumental for adapting to the changing context and practice, thereby enabling effective leadership. The narratives and case studies presented a narrative that demonstrated the relationship between dynamic, forward-thinking professional learning and the nurturing of adept leadership. This chapter has reinforced the critical importance of professional learning as a mechanism for nurturing and maintaining robust leadership. As the ECEC sector continues to evolve, marked by fresh theoretical insights, methodological advances, policy shifts, and novel management strategies, the commitment to continuous professional growth stands as the bedrock of successful leadership development.

Reflective activities

Reflect on the 'Early childhood leaders of the future' box above. Can you identify skills and knowledge you could ideally develop?
Examine the learning framework and map out your intentions for learning.

References

Adriano, M. N. & Rosa, E. D. (2023). A proposed framework for designing adult education programs from the perspectives of adult education professionals. *International Journal of Education, Technology and Science, 3*(1), 87–109.

Australian Children's Education & Care Quality Authority. (2023). *Guide to the NQF* https://www.acecqa.gov.au/nqf/about/guide

Australian Children's Education & Care Quality Authority. (2020). *Progressing a national approach to the children's education and care workforce* [Workforce report November 2019]. https://www.acecqa.gov.au/sites/default/files/2020-10/ChildrensEducationandCareNationalWorkforceStrategy_0.pdf

Bloom, P. J. & Bella, J. (2005). Investment in leadership training—The payoff for early childhood education. *Young Children, 60*(1), 32–40. https://www.jstor.org/stable/42729176

Bøe, M., Kristiansen, E. & Rydjord Tholin, K. (2023). Case-based leadership learning: How to improve work-related stress in early childhood education centre directors. *Teachers and Teaching, 29*(2), 180–194. https://doi.org/10.1080/13540602.2022.2155808

Denee, R. (2018). Professional learning and distributed leadership: A symbiotic relationship. *The New Zealand Annual Review of Education, 23*, 63–78. https://doi.org/10.26686/nzaroe.v23i0.5284

Ebbeck, M. & Waniganayake, M. (2003). *Early childhood professionals: Leading today and tomorrow.* MacLennan + Petty.

Department for Education. (2024). *Early years qualification requirements and standards*. Department for Education United Kingdom. https://www.gov.uk/government/publications/early-years-qualification-requirements-and-standards

Education Council. (2018). *The leadership strategy for the teaching profession of Aotearoa New Zealand: Enabling every teacher to develop their leadership capability.* https://teachingcouncil.nz/professional-practice/rauhuia-leadership-space-home/rauhuia-leadership-space/leadership-strategy/

Fonsén, E. & Soukainen, U. (2020). Sustainable pedagogical leadership in Finnish early childhood education (ECE): An evaluation by ECE professionals. *Early Childhood Education Journal. 48*(2), 213–222. https://doi.org/10.1007/s10643-019-00984-y

Gibbs, L. (2020). "That's your right as a human isn't it?" The emergence and development of leading as a socially-just practice in early childhood education. *Australasian Journal of Early Childhood, 45*(4), 295–308. https://doi.org/10.1177/1836939120966093

Gibbs, L. (2022). Leadership emergence and development: Organizations shaping leading in early childhood education. *Educational Management Administration & Leadership, 50*(4), 672–693. https://doi.org/10.1177/1741143220940324

Gibbs, L., Press, F. & Wong, S. (2019). Compliance in a landscape of complexity: Regulation and educational leadership. In L. Gibbs & M. Gasper (Eds), *Challenging the intersection of policy with pedagogy* (pp. 159–174). Routledge.

Greve, A. & Hansen, O. H. (2018). Toddlers in Nordic early childhood education and care. In M. Fleer & B. van Oers (Eds), *International handbook of early childhood education* (pp. 907–927). Springer. https://doi.org/10.1007/978-94-024-0927-7_47

Jorde Bloom, P. (2016). *Measuring work attitudes: Technical manual for the Early Childhood Job Satisfaction Survey and Early Childhood Work Environment Survey.* New Horizons.

Knowles, M. S., Holton, E. F. & Swanson, R. A. (2014). *The adult learner: The definitive classic in adult education and human resource development.* Routledge.

Layen, S. (2015). Do reflections on personal autobiography as captured in narrated life-stories illuminate leadership development in the field of early childhood? *Professional Development in Education, 41*(2), 273–289. https://doi.org/10.1080/19415257.2014.986814

McCormick Center for Early Childhood Leadership. (2014). *Taking Charge of Change.* https://mccormickcenter.nl.edu/library/taking-charge-of-change-20-year-report/

Nicholson, J. & Kroll, L. (2015). Developing leadership for early childhood professionals through oral inquiry: Strengthening equity through making particulars visible in dilemmas of practice. *Early Child Development and Care, 185*(1), 17–43. https://doi.org/10.1080/03004430.2014.903939

Nicholson, J., Kuhl, K., Maniates, H., Lin, B. & Bonetti, S. (2018). A review of the literature on leadership in early childhood: Examining epistemological foundations and considerations of social justice. *Early Child Development and Care, 190*(2), 91–122. https://doi.org/10.1080/03004430.2018.1455036

OECD. (2019). Providing Quality Early Childhood Education and Care: Results from the Starting Strong Survey 2018. OECD Publishing. https://doi.org/10.1787/301005d1-en

Productivity Commission. (2011). *Early childhood development workforce* [Productivity Commission research report]. https://www.pc.gov.au/inquiries/completed/education-workforce-early-childhood/report/early-childhood-report.pdf

Rodd, J. (2012). Building leadership expertise of future early childhood professionals. *Journal of Early Childhood Teacher Education, 22*(1), 9–12. https://doi.org/10.1080/10901027.2001.10486430

Talan, T. & Bloom, P. J. (2004). *Program administration scale: Measuring early childhood leadership and management.* Teachers College Press.

Talan, T., Bloom, P. J. & Kelton, R. (2014). Building the leadership capacity of early childhood directors: An evaluation of a leadership development model. *Early Childhood Research & Practice, 16*(1&2), Special Section, article 1. https://ecrp.illinois.edu/v16n1/talan.html

Thornton, K. (2010). Lessons for leadership development: What we can learn from the UK. *Journal of Educational Leadership, Policy and Practice, 25*(2), 29–40. https://search.informit.org/doi/10.3316/informit.554493887096660

Waniganayake, M., Cheeseman, S., Fenech, M., Hadley, F. & Shepherd, W. (2023). *Leadership: Contexts and complexities in early childhood education* (3rd ed.). Oxford University Press.

Waniganayake, M. & Stipanovic, S. (2016). Advancing leadership capacity: Preparation of early childhood leaders in Australia through a coursework Masters degree. *Journal of Early Childhood Education Research, 5*(2), Special Issue), 268–288. https://journal.fi/jecer/article/view/114061

7 | A Path Ahead

This chapter

- explores the path ahead for emerging and positional leaders
- highlights the positive outlook for early childhood leaders
- shares stories of inspiring leadership in others, optimism, joy, commitment and hope
- recounts the message of this book

Introduction

This concluding chapter discusses the path ahead for emerging and positional leaders. Despite the challenges and complexity of leading in early childhood education and care (ECEC), there is much optimism, joy and inspiration gained through work that transforms and contributes to a 'world worth living in' (Kemmis et al., 2014). An increased focus internationally on the importance of childhood and early childhood development bodes well for emerging and positional leaders who work within ECEC organisations.

DOI: 10.4324/9781003277590-11

A story of leadership resilience

> *In my leadership, I'm most proud of my resilience, I think, in such a rapidly and evolving sector. You have to be resilient. And I think coming, trying to overcome those hurdles and challenges along the way just makes you a stronger person. I think a team approach is really important for leadership, and I'm really proud of what we have created at our workplace and our kindness to everyone. You must have openness.*
>
> —Kim, Study 2

Thinking ahead: A positive outlook for those who lead

The path ahead for leading and leadership in early childhood education and care (ECEC) is filled with optimism, joy, commitment and motivation, which promise the opportunity to influence outcomes for young children, the ECEC profession and the community where families live and work. There are many reasons for this optimism.

Recognition of the importance of ECEC

Governments increasingly recognise the critical importance of early childhood education (ECE). Research consistently shows that quality early learning experiences have a profound effect on children's cognitive, social and emotional development, and leadership has a profound effect on process quality (Douglass, 2019). As a result, there is a growing commitment to investing in the ECEC sector.

Innovative teaching practices

Early childhood educators are embracing innovative teaching practices driven by a commitment to providing the best possible learning experiences for children. From incorporating technology in developmentally appropriate ways to employing play-based and child-centred experiences, educators are continuously seeking creative solutions to enhance early learning. There is

A Path Ahead

still the opportunity to lead the resistance to instructional learning and punitive assessment of young children (Archer, 2022).

Professional learning

The field of early childhood educational leadership has evolved to place a strong emphasis on professional development. Emerging leaders are starting to access development opportunities, including advanced degree programs, mentorship opportunities and specialised training; for example, in Sweden, preschool managers have become principals, and they now have access to the Principal Program (Lund, 2022). These avenues for growth ensure that the new generations of leaders are well prepared to meet the evolving needs of young children, the profession and the broader community.

Advocacy and policy reform

Leaders in ECE are increasingly engaging in advocacy efforts and influencing policy reform. Their collective voices are helping to secure more significant investments in the field, leading to improved working conditions, better compensation for educators and greater access to quality programs for children from all backgrounds. For example, in Canada, advocacy for child care is driven by the recognition that universal, publicly funded and managed child care is essential. The childcare movement emphasises the need for all children, regardless of their location in Canada, to have access to regulated, affordable, inclusive, culturally safe, flexible and high-quality early learning and child care from birth to age 12. By leveraging the federal government's allocated budgets and legislative authority, leaders aim to create a future where every child's needs are met and where child care is recognised as a vital part of our social safety net. This advocacy extends to supporting early childhood educators in obtaining fair living wages, considering that 97% of early childcare educators are women. Strengthening mental health support for frontline child and youth workers is also critical, given the effect of workforce sustainability on the quality of care (Canadian Child Care Federation, 2024).

Yet advocacy and leadership are enacted in everyday practice. This extract from Theresa, highlighted in the introduction to Part III, shows that the motivation and drive to continuously improve enable the development of high-quality ECEC:

> *I think it's that constantly wanting to do things better. We talk about greatness, but there is no such thing as greatness. There is, just for me, that drive to want to evolve and make changes and do things better, and how can we evolve this practice, and what can we look at to make things better for ourselves, to have that passion not die for the children and families within our service, and for the wider community.*
>
> —Theresa, Study 1

Inclusion and equity

A growing commitment to inclusivity and equity in ECE means that leaders are working to ensure that every child, regardless of their background or abilities, has access to high-quality educational opportunities. Initiatives that aim to reduce disparities and provide support for marginalised communities are on the rise. Yet leading is present in the everyday actions of educators who advocate for children:

> *That's what families and communities deserve. I will go that extra mile for you, and you don't need to give me anything. I'm going to do it because that's what you deserve. That's your right as a human, isn't it?*
>
> (Gibbs, 2020, p. 301)

Family and community engagement

Early childhood leaders recognise the vital role that families and communities play in a child's education and well-being. Efforts to build strong partnerships with families and communities strengthen the foundation of early education and create a comprehensive and effective support system for young children.

Increasing recognition of the field's significance, the focus on professional development, innovative teaching practices, advocacy and policy reform, inclusivity and equity and the emphasis on engaging families and communities contribute to a positive future for ECE and, therefore, children.

A Path Ahead

Optimism: The cultivation of leaders

There are many reasons to be optimistic about leadership development in ECEC. They include an increasing research focus on the emergence of leadership and greater diversity in approaches to leadership development.

Increasing focus on leadership research

A trend in early childhood leadership research is the shift from a traditional, hierarchical and individualistic view of leadership to a more collaborative, distributed and relational view of leadership (Douglass, 2018; Gibbs, 2022). This reflects the recognition that leadership is a practice—not a fixed position or role but a dynamic and contextual practice that involves multiple actors and interactions within and across early childhood settings.

Leadership is concerned not only with management and administration but also with pedagogy, curriculum and advocacy. Therefore, early childhood leadership research aims to explore and understand the complex and diverse aspects and dimensions of leadership in early childhood and how they influence the quality of education and care for children, families and communities (Gibbs, 2021).

There are, however, challenges within the field of leadership research, as highlighted in Chapter 1. These challenges include the lack of a clear and consistent definition and conceptualisation of leadership, the diversity and variability of early childhood settings and contexts, the limited availability and accessibility of data and resources, and the ethical and methodological issues involved in conducting research with young children and practitioners (Dunlop, 2008; Siraj-Blatchford & Manni, 2007). Further research is needed to identify what effective and 'good' leadership looks like to gain perspectives from a range of stakeholders. Emerging and positional leaders hold significant knowledge from their experience as ECEC professionals over time:

> What does 'good' leadership look like?
> Passion, qualifications, and that commitment to professional lifelong learning is really important because there is new research emerging every day, you know, how can we keep improving on our practice. I just don't mean caring and nurturing, but there are times

when you need to have strength to deal with some really difficult situations.

I think a good leader is knowing when to put up a hand and ask for help because it is sometimes lonely and thankless and a difficult job.

I think, too, being part of a professional organisation. I mean, I think about my career. I was actively encouraged to join ECA [Early Childhood Australia] as a young woman. I just thought, 'Oh, my goodness, I don't think I can hack this.' But I persevered; I met some fantastic mentors/encouragers. They probably didn't even know they were doing it. Over that journey, I had opportunities to be exposed to different ways of doing and thinking.

Being part of a professional organisation and the ability to network, outside of your comfort zone, not just insular. It's not about thinking, 'I have to do all of that', but being able to ask a question, 'I'm not sure how to handle this'. You must use those networks to help you in your leadership program. I think being a CEO, it's just a title. Some people get caught up in the status and the title. For me, that's never been an issue. I fell into this job. I didn't necessarily apply for it, but fell into it, but I've grown into it, and I've loved it.

–Ros, Study 1

Early childhood leadership research faces the pressure and expectations to inform and influence policy and practice and to demonstrate the effects and outcomes of leadership on children's learning and development (Siraj et al., 2023), but research must also embed practices for leadership sustainability.

Greater impetus and diversity in leadership development

Because they recognise that effective leadership is fundamental to providing high-quality education and care for young children and their families, ECEC leaders influence critical aspects of ECEC.

ECEC emerging and positional leaders directly influence the growth, learning and overall well-being of children. Their decisions and practices shape the educational experiences that lay the foundation for high-quality education

A Path Ahead

and care. Effective leadership contributes to staff morale, job satisfaction and professional growth. When leaders create supportive environments, educators are more likely to remain committed to their roles (Personal communication, 2023).

Emerging and positional leaders foster collaborative relationships with families and communities. Involving parents and caregivers creates a sense of belonging and shared responsibility for children's development. Emerging and positional leaders in ECEC drive innovation through evaluation and refining teaching practices, planning and programming and learning frameworks. Leaders' insights influence policy decisions that affect the entire sector.

Several factors underscore the urgency of leadership development in ECEC. Leaders navigate diverse contexts and respond to the unique needs and rights of children, families and communities from various backgrounds and abilities. The work of the leader has become more complex and demanding. Additionally, increasing standards demand evidence-based practices. Leaders must implement effective strategies, assess outcomes and demonstrate the value of ECEC for children and communities. Workforce shortages, turnover and professionalisation also pose challenges and require emerging and positional leaders to motivate staff, advocate for the profession and implement equitable access to quality ECEC.

Investing in leadership development is critical. Researchers, practitioners and policy-makers must collaborate to nurture the emergence and cultivation of leading and leadership.

Joy

Despite the challenges of leading, joy and pride in the role are clear. This joy stems from the experience of being with children and educators, sharing moments of fun and reflecting on successes.

Recent research on joy in ECEC highlights the importance of spontaneity for educators and leaders (Karjalainen et al., 2019). Karjalainen et al. found that teachers and children share joyful moments that lead to meaningful dialogues. Rather than being meticulously planned, these dialogical, joyful encounters emerge spontaneously from daily interactions. Similarly, in Study 2, leaders recognised and valued these moments as opportunities to build respectful relationships with children and educators.

> *I love being with the children. I love that satisfaction and joy of working with the children. And you know, having belly laughs every day. Because kids are funny, you know, they say the funniest things, they do the funniest things, and just watching their development and their growth. It's just really, really exciting. But I'm really struggling with it. So I'm going to just teach one day a week next year, which I think would be good because also that may be the children but dedicate more time to leadership. And I think the only reason why teaching directing has worked for me is because my team is incredible. They are just the most amazing, passionate team of educators.*
>
> —Sara, Study 2

> ### Where do you find joy and pride in leading?
>
> *I guess I help people flourish. I guess that's what I'm proud of because I can see that that's happened with people that I've worked with, seeing them go their path and flourish in and thrive in what they're doing.*
>
> —Kim M, Study 2

> *I really enjoy having conversations with people and so, when my colleagues do come to me with the sort of questions I really enjoy, sort of bouncing back a question back to them, or when they explain that perspective, trying to unpack that a little bit more, or sharing my own perspective, and the reasons behind my thoughts on my experiences as well.*
>
> —Loretta, Study 2

Commitment and motivation

Leaders who are deeply committed to their roles demonstrate dedication to the well-being and development of children. Their commitment extends beyond administrative tasks; it encompasses a genuine passion for fostering

A Path Ahead

positive environments. When leaders prioritise commitment, they model persistence, resilience and a sense of purpose. This commitment resonates with educators, families and the broader community, creating a cohesive network that places children at the heart of decision-making. By embodying commitment, leaders inspire trust, encourage collaboration and drive continuous improvement in ECEC settings (Gibbs, 2020, 2022).

Further, motivated leaders ignite enthusiasm and drive among their teams. They recognise that their influence extends beyond paperwork and policies. Instead, they focus on empowering educators, acknowledging their expertise and providing growth opportunities. Motivated leaders actively seek out innovative practices and stay abreast of research and trends. Their enthusiasm is contagious, and this encourages educators to explore new teaching methods, engage in reflective practices and create dynamic learning environments. By fostering motivation, leaders elevate the quality of ECE, which ensures that every child receives the best possible start in their educational journey.

In conversation with leaders: What keeps you motivated with the strength to go on?

> *I think I have a tenacity to keep chipping away. Keep chipping away at those really small things that we know is so important. I have the passion. I have the strong relational commitment to children and families.*
> *—Cerise, Study 2*

> *There are things that I hold dear. My values. My flexibility. I won't compromise.*
> *—Rebecca, Study 2*

> *One of my values is to give each staff member time to time and time to breathe. I think the biggest reason why I'm here is my practice in allowing children to be themselves and not be afraid of being judged or about being different. This has to extend to educators.*
> *—Belinda, Study 2*

> *I work towards building and having a real open communication amongst each other, and, as well, encouraging those more robust discussions that in the past people would have avoided having one another for fear of conflict.*
>
> –Darrell, Study 2

In conclusion

This book began with the troubles and challenges of leadership emergence and development with a comprehensive exploration of the empirical research on leadership in ECEC. A historical context and theories and practices were examined to offer insights into the current state of ECEC leadership, and you were encouraged to think differently about leadership conceptualisations. Leadership was proposed as a relational activity that emphasises collective responsibility for the education and care of children, educators and families rather than solely pursuing organisational goals.

At the next stage of this book, the complexity of emerging and positional leaders' knowledge, skills and values and the ECEC environments where leadership is enacted was illuminated. The illumination of this complexity was fundamental as a platform for discussing leadership development.

In the third and final part of the book, an imperative for leadership development as a collective organisational responsibility is expressed. This responsibility is framed within organisational arrangements that shape leadership practices, including cultural-discursive, material-economic and social-political elements (Kemmis et al., 2014). This shaping also comprised the organisation's learning culture to adapt to changing contexts and enhance leadership effectiveness to describe how effective leadership practices could be enabled and shaped.

This book's overarching theme and enduring message is that leadership in ECEC is a practice open to many rather than an individualistic, unsustainable positional role. It also highlights the influential role of leaders in advocating for high-quality ECEC environments and the community, moving away from the traditional view of the solitary, heroic leader. The message is also that the responsibility for leadership cultivation lies with ECEC organisations, and this development is more than a training program. Cultivation is a matter of holistic development within an organisation. It is, however,

A Path Ahead

critical to highlight the promise with which leadership emergence and cultivation go forward within the ECEC field and profession.

And now… a closing story of leading

This book began with my own story of leadership, of being stirred into the practices of leading while feeling confused, perplexed and disoriented. As an inexperienced positional leader, I longed for a collective way to lead that could result in positive outcomes for children and families. Over time, my ideas changed, but the complexity remained.

The privilege I had, therefore, to step away from a key role to study leading became an opportunity to learn about my own leadership practices. I discovered that my practices were inefficient and consumed with the burden of overwhelming responsibility. Such practices constrained my own and others' self-determination as individuals within a collective (Kemmis et al., 2014). By studying leadership, I developed new knowledge and transformed my practices, and this created in me a changed disposition for leadership.

Over the past few years, I have shared my learning and worked collaboratively with ECEC leaders. We developed our knowledge and skills together. I presented unfamiliar conceptualisations of leadership and leading and observed how these transformed the perceptions of reluctant emerging leaders. The notion that leading could be a socially just practice helped educators understand that leadership could influence rather than control. I breathed a sigh of relief collectively with positional leaders when we learned together that ECEC leaders did not have to perform heroic actions and be endlessly decisive and certain. Through an analytical lens, I saw that organisational structures and arrangements could facilitate leadership cultivation and development. I came to understand that complexity was the natural state of an early childhood organisation, where disruption leads to creativity, innovation and emergence. With newfound knowledge, I stepped into another positional leadership role.

Then came Covid-19. If I needed an environment in which to test new knowledge and skills, this was it! The environment was complex, disruptive and constantly changing. Starting my new role and the onset of the pandemic coincided. I, therefore, had inadequate knowledge of the organisation's regular operation and practices of leading. Instead of lamenting the past, we, as a team, adapted and transformed together. The team shared the value of the pursuit of high-quality ECE. Our hopes for workforce sustainability and educator and child well-being drove our collaborative efforts. Our work was shaped by the traditions and culture of the organisation and by the conditions of the pandemic and environmental disasters close by. This work was also shaped by my own new knowledge and transformation.

> In this ever-changing world, things do not stand still, frozen in a social tableaux. As we are equally well aware, change is happening all the time in a dance between identity and otherness, a dance between the reproduction of some things alongside the transformation of others.
>
> (Kemmis et al., 2014, p. 2)

I now value disruption and complexity. Complexity generates innovation, creativity and the potential for leadership emergence. I am no longer as decisive and certain. The lack of certainty creates new opportunities for others and for the direction of our work within ECE.

—Leanne

Reflective question

There is only one more question for readers of this chapter and this book: Where to, from here, in cultivating and developing leading and leadership in ECEC organisations and settings?

> *When I first started out, my world was very black and white, and I think leadership has taught me all the colours in between.*
>
> –Kim, Study 2

References

Archer, N. (2022). 'I have this subversive curriculum underneath': Narratives of micro resistance in early childhood education. *Journal of Early Childhood Research,* *20*(3), 431–445. https://doi.org/10.1177/1476718X211059907

A Path Ahead

Canadian Child Care Federation. (2024). *Support us: Advocate*. https://cccf-fcsge.ca/get-involved/support-us/advocate/

Douglass, A. (2018). Redefining leadership: Lessons from an early education leadership development initiative. *Early Childhood Education Journal, 46*(4), 387–396. https://doi.org/10.1007/s10643-017-0871-9

Douglass, A. (2019). Leadership for quality early childhood education and care. *OECD Education Working Paper* (No. 211). OECD Publishing. https://doi.org/10.1787/6e563bae-en

Dunlop, A. (2008). *A literature review on leadership in the early years*. Learning and Teaching Scotland. Website archived 6 April 2011: https://web.archive.org/web/20110406050458/http:/www.ltscotland.org.uk/publications/a/leadershippreview.asp?strReferringChannel=&strReferringPageID=tcm:4-623087-64

Gibbs, L. (2020). "That's your right as a human isn't it?" The emergence and development of leading as a socially-just practice in early childhood education. *Australasian Journal of Early Childhood, 45*(4), 295–308. https://doi.org/10.1177/1836939120966093

Gibbs, L. (2021). *Leadership-as-practice in early childhood education and care settings*. Early Childhood Australia. https://www.earlychildhoodaustralia.org.au/our-publications/research-practice-series/research-practice-series-index/2021-issues/leadership-as-practice-in-early-childhood-education-and-care-settings/

Gibbs, L. (2022). Leadership emergence and development: Organizations shaping leading in early childhood education. *Educational Management Administration & Leadership, 50*(4), 672–693. https://doi.org/10.1177/1741143220940324

Karjalainen, S., Hanhimäki, E. & Puroila, A. M. (2019). Dialogues of joy: Shared moments of joy between teachers and children in early childhood education settings. *International Journal of Early Childhood, 51*(2), 129–143. https://doi.org/10.1007/s13158-019-00244-5

Kemmis, S., Wilkinson, J., Edwards-Groves, C., Hardy, I., Grootenboer, P. & Bristol, L. (2014). Praxis, practice and practice architectures. In S. Kemmis, J. Wilkinson, C. Edwards-Groves, I. Hardy, P. Grootenboer & L. Bristol (Eds), *Changing practices, changing education* (pp. 25–41). Springer.

Lund, S. (2022). The geographic periphery as architecture for leadership practice with Swedish primary school principals: A peripatetic leading practice. *International Journal of Leadership in Education*. https://doi.org/10.1080/13603124.2022.2027526

Siraj, I., Melhuish, E., Howard, S. J., Neilsen-Hewett, C., Kingston, D., De Rosnay M., Huang, R., Gardiner, J. & Luu, B. (2023). Improving quality of teaching and child development: A randomised controlled trial of the leadership for learning intervention in preschools. *Frontiers in Psychology, 13*. https://doi.org/10.3389/fpsyg.2022.1092284

Siraj-Blatchford, I. & Manni, L. (2007). *Effective leadership in the early years sector: The ELEYS study*. Institute of Education, University of London.

Appendix
Research Studies

Study 1

Summary of the study

Study 1 addressed the challenges of early childhood education and care (ECEC) leadership cultivation and generated new possibilities for the emergence and development of leading within ECEC organisations.

The research investigated the phenomena of emerging leadership and the development of leading of 24 (originally 30) educators in three Australian early childhood education (ECE) sites (Table A.1).

Mini-ethnographic case study was employed as the methodology for the research study. Methods comprised fieldwork using direct observation, including a leadership observation tool (Table A.2) and unstructured interviews, document analysis and dialogic cafés. The gathering of data and subsequent analysis were conducted within a framework of the theory of practice architectures.

The research findings supported the re-conceptualisation of leadership as a dynamic collective practice, open to everyone. This practice acts as a foundation for positional leadership roles and contributes to the achievement of high-quality ECE. The findings identified the distinct arrangements of language and culture, physical space, resource allocation and social relationships that support the cultivation of such leadership. Findings also indicate that organisations should resist a formulaic approach to leadership development. Instead, they can focus on the cultural-discursive, material-economic and social-political arrangements for leadership cultivation and development whilst considering the unique influence their governance practices and traditions can make to leadership development (adapted from Gibbs, 2021).

Participant summary

Table A.1 Study 1 participants

Site	Participant	Role	Positional	Emerging	Qualifications	Years of experience	Years within site
Robson Early Childhood Education Centre	1	Educator		X	Certificate III	7	1
	2	Educator		X	Certificate III	2	2
	3	Educator		X	Diploma	4	2
	4	Educator		X	Diploma / B Ed (ECE/UG)	4	2
	5	Educator / Room Leader	X		Diploma	12	3
	6	Educator / Room Leader	X		Diploma	20	5
	7	ECT / Educational Leader	X		Early Childhood Teacher	10	1
	8	Centre Director	X		Diploma / Management Dip	5	2
	9	Manager	X		B Ed (ECE)	25	10
	10	Manager	X		B Ed (ECE) Grad Dip	25	20
	11	CEO	X		B Ed (ECE)	40	30

(Continued)

Table A.1 (Continued)

Site	Participant	Role	Positional	Emerging	Qualifications	Years of experience	Years within site
Discovery Early Learning Centre	12	Educator		X	Certificate III	4	3
	13	Educator		X	Certificate III / B Ed Prim (UG)	6	2
	14	Teacher		X	B Ed (ECE) (UG)	3	>1
	15	Educator / Room Leader	X		Diploma	5	2
	16	ECT / Outdoor Leader	X		B Ed (ECE)	8	3
	17	ECT / Educational Leader	X		B Ed (ECE) / Fine Arts	10	4
	18	Centre Director	X		Certificate III / B Sports Management	6	5
	19	CEO	X		B Ed (ECE)	25	20
Rondure Preschool	20	Educator		X	Certificate III	24	10
	21	Educator		X	Diploma	28	16
	22	ECT		X	B Ed (ECE)	20	6
	23	Centre Director	X		B Ed (ECE)	26	4
	24	Manager	X		B Ed (ECE)	30	10
Total	**24**		**14**	**10**			

B Ed, bachelor of education degree; B Ed Prim, bachelor of primary education degree; Dip, diploma; ECE, early childhood education; ECT, early childhood teacher; UG, undergraduate.

Questions	Could be present in arrangements of	Could be observed in practices (but are not limited to)			
		Siraj-Blatchford and Manni (2007)	Coleman et al. (2016)	Standards	Hazy and Uhl-Bien (2015)
What personal, professional and organisational language and communication enhance the emergence and development of leading and leadership in early childhood education and care (ECEC) sites?	Enabling leadership (as defined by Marion and Gonzales, 2013).	Ensure shared understandings, meanings and goals. Communicate well.	Engaging responsively	Communicate well.	Articulate an idealised future with shared values and aspirations. Ask each person to invest their energy and resources in the organisation. Clarify in-group/out-group boundaries, perhaps by using 'us' versus 'them' language.
What are the networks of professional relationships and communication that boost leading and leadership?	Adaptive leadership (as defined by Marion and Gonzales 2013).	Identify and articulate a collective vision. Communicate well.	Clear vision. Understanding of ECEC.	Communicate well. Commit to ongoing professional development. Encourage critical reflection. Statement of philosophy.	Community-building. Initiate and perform inclusion rituals like group celebrations. Bring diverse experiences and perspectives together and support differences of opinion. Form small teams and rotate membership often to break up stale thinking.

(*Continued*)

Questions	Could be present in arrangements of	Could be observed in practices (but are not limited to)			
		Siraj-Blatchford and Manni (2007)	Coleman et al. (2016)	Standards	Hazy and Uhl-Bien (2015)
What personal, professional and organisational resources enhance the emergence of leading and leadership in ECEC sites?	Administrative leadership (as defined by Marion and Gonzales, 2013).	Builds learning community. Builds team culture.	Motivating staff. Uses business skills strategically.	Effectively documented policies and procedures. Appropriate governance arrangements. Establish and maintain administrative systems.	Make people feel they are part of something valued and significant. Use resource allocation authority to 'kill' dead-end projects or wasteful activities. Establish specific task targets, dependencies and deliverables. Provide resources and space to try new things and new directions. Encourage broad adoption of innovations that have been vetted. Build trust that individuals will have access to shared resources.
What skills, understandings and dispositions underpin the development of leading and leadership?	Cultural-discursive, material-economic, social-political. Enable leadership (as defined by Marion and Gonzales, 2013).	Communicate well. Contextual literacy. Critical reflection. Commitment to ongoing professional development. Builds team culture encourages and builds community partnership. Uses evidence to drive improvement and outcomes.	Contextual literacy. Embracing integrated working. Engaging responsively. Committed to own and others' learning. Motivating and coaching staff.	The induction of educators, coordinators and staff members. Commitment to continuous improvement. Performance of educators, coordinators and staff members is evaluated, and individual development plans are in place.	Encourage openness to surprises to learn / do not punish failure. Provide clear roles, task-specific training and follow up on expected activities.

Appendix

Study 2

Summary of the study

Study 2 was a six-month community of practice involving 16 participants divided into two groups, each comprising eight individuals with diverse experience, skills and knowledge. The groups convened monthly for two-hour sessions. The study employed the dialogic café method, a participatory approach designed to facilitate collective dialogue and learning. The dialogic café is a structured conversation that democratically creates knowledge for collaborative learning (Fouché & Light, 2011; Jorgenson & Steier, 2013). The event is hosted rather than 'facilitated'. In the dialogic café, themes are emergent, power is shared, and learning is collaborative (Steier, et al., 2015). Each session began with a provocation inspired by reading. The sessions were based on the *World Café Guide* below.

The investigation considered how positional leaders conceptualise and define 'leadership' and how they encourage emergence of leading. We considered what innovative practices create the conditions for leadership emergence and development. Additionally, an examination of leading through critical times was conducted.

Complexity leadership theory and the theory of practice architectures provided the theoretical frames for the study. Together, the theories account for the complexity of ECE leadership and maintain a strong link with practice. Both theories encompass emergence, self-organisation, complex environments, universal leadership development and interdependence of practices (Uhl-Bien & Arena, 2017; Wilkinson & Kemmis, 2014).

Outcomes of the study included the recognition of innovative practice within ECE organisations enabling leadership emergence and development, an illumination of the histories and experiences of emerging and positional leaders and the characteristics of leadership during times of crisis.

Participant summary

Participants were ECE professionals interested in leadership emergence and cultivation. They were not required to hold a position of leadership. However, they were required to hold a position within an ECE organisation as an educator, administrator, manager, professional development leader or support staff.

Appendix

Table A.3 Study 2 participants

Participant	Role	Positional	Emerging	Years of experience	Years in role
1	Centre director	X		23	5
2	Centre director	X		29	20
3	Centre director	X		30	6.5
4	Centre director	X		27.5	4
5	Centre director	X		15	5
6	Program Manager	X		40	7
7	Centre director	X		30	17
8	Early childhood teacher		X	15	1
9	Program Manager	X		28	6
10	Centre director	X		29	11
11	Centre director	X		14	14
12	Centre director	X		20	3
13	Centre director	X		30	18
14	Centre director	X		30	2
15	Centre director	X		30	8
16	Early childhood teacher		X	5	2

The Dialogic Café

The following information on the Dialogic Café was shared with participants prior to the commencement of the study. This method was used in Study 1 and Study 2.

What is a Dialogic/World Café?

The method of World Café is emergent by design. An initial 'provocation' sets the scene, but questions are raised by participants, and there are no preconceived lines of investigation. The *Design Principles of the World Café* (Foundation, 2017) will be used in the research. These principles have been used in research projects that have met ethics requirements.

166

Appendix

Design Principles of the World Café

1) Set the Context: Pay attention to the reason you are bringing people together and what you want to achieve. Knowing the purpose and parameters of your meeting enables you to consider and choose the most important elements to realize your goals (e.g., who should be part of the conversation, what themes or questions will be most pertinent, and what sorts of harvest will be more useful).

2) Create a Hospitable Online Space: Café hosts around the world emphasise the power and importance of creating a hospitable space—one that feels safe and inviting. When people feel comfortable to be themselves, they do their most creative thinking, speaking and listening. Consider how your invitation and your physical set-up contribute to creating a welcoming atmosphere.

3) Explore Questions that Matter: Knowledge emerges in response to compelling questions. Find questions that are relevant to the real-life concerns of the group. Powerful questions that "travel well" help attract collective energy, insight and action as they move throughout a system. Depending on the time frame available and your objectives, your Café may explore a single question or use a progressively deeper line of inquiry through several conversational rounds.

4) Encourage Everyone's Contribution: As leaders, we are increasingly aware of the importance of participation, but most people don't only want to participate, they want to actively contribute to making a difference. It is important to encourage everyone in your meeting to contribute their ideas and perspectives, and be sure to allow anyone who wants to participate by simply listening to do so.

5) Connect Diverse Perspectives: The opportunity to move between groups, meet new people, actively contribute your thinking, and link the essence of your discoveries to ever-widening circles of thought is one of the distinguishing characteristics of the Café. As participants carry key ideas or themes to new groups, they exchange perspectives, greatly enriching the possibility for surprising new insights.

6) Listen Together for Patterns and Insights: The quality of our listening is perhaps the most important factor determining the success of a Café. Through practicing shared listening and paying attention to themes, patterns and insights, we begin to sense a connection to the larger whole.

Appendix

Encourage people to listen for what is not being spoken along with what is being shared.

7) Share Collective Discoveries: Conversations held in one group reflect a pattern of wholeness that connects with the conversations with other groups. The last phase of the Café, often called the 'harvest', involves making this pattern of wholeness visible to everyone in a large group conversation. Invite a few minutes of silent reflection on the patterns, themes and deeper questions experienced in the small group conversations and call them out to share with the larger group.

Study 3

Summary of the study

The following summary describes the study methods and identifies the number of participants in Study 3. The study outcomes are incorporated into this book but have not been extensively applied or explicated.

The research study used a case study methodology (Yin, 2012) to investigate how an ECEC organisation fosters and supports leadership and innovation for a 'future-ready' workforce. This approach was chosen because it allows for a detailed study of leadership and innovation within a unique organisational context.

The research was primarily qualitative, aiming to investigate perceptions, interpretation and understanding. A systematic approach was planned to ensure the dependability of the individual case study and allow for transferability.

The research methods were selected to address a practical research problem with methods that would yield as much valuable data for the organisation as possible. The approach was philosophically and theoretically aligned with organisational vision and values and with the intentions and research questions for the project.

Survey (529 respondents): An online survey consisting of 25 questions was conducted. The survey included nine multiple-choice questions and 12 Likert scale questions. There was also an option to comment on key topics of leadership attributes and approaches to leadership within the organisation.

Structured and Semi-Structured Interviews (55 participants): These interviews aimed to elicit unique responses and stories that were important

Appendix

in building a descriptive case study. The interviews were carried out with the executive team, CEO and a board member.

Focus Groups (four groups): Focus groups were used to interview a group with common experiences in a relatively unstructured way. These groups were constructed with 2 to 10 participants in regional areas and the cities of Melbourne and Sydney.

Dialogic/World Café events (five sites): This collaborative method engages participants in dialogue around critical questions. The World Café events elicited unique and innovative responses.

Guided reflective inquiry: conducted over six months. **Nine participants** completed all required reflective events and writings. This method was particularly apt as leadership development benefits from critical reflection. Participants answered evolving questions through written exercises focusing on organisational support for leadership. Their writings were shared with researchers. The sessions covered leadership and workforce development and innovation. Internal documents, programs and policies were analysed to understand how systems and dedicated programs influence these areas within the organisation. Additionally, leadership programs from various organisations were examined to compare leadership cultivation methods.

A number of opportunities were highlighted as a result of findings in the research study. The development of an organisational workforce narrative would encourage ongoing education. Leadership and innovation could be integral to strategic plans, and resources allocated for development. Career planning could involve structured yet reflective processes helping employees understand their growth path within the organisation. A shared leadership language, rooted in ECE philosophy, could be established, along with employees committed to integrating this language into their communication and leadership actions. Leadership development for directors includes training in administration, management and leadership tailored to their existing skills and knowledge.

References

Coleman, A., Sharp, C., & Handscomb, G. (2016). Leading highly performing children's centres: Supporting the development of the 'accidental leaders'. *Educational Management Administration & Leadership, 44*(5), 775–793. https://doi.org/10.1177/1741143215574506

Appendix

Fouché, C., & Light, G. (2011). An invitation to dialogue: 'The World Café' in social work research. *Qualitative Social Work, 10*(1), 28–48. http://doi.org/10.1177/1473325010376016

Gibbs, L. (2021). *Leadership-as-practice in early childhood education and care settings*. Early Childhood Australia. https://www.earlychildhoodaustralia.org.au/our-publications/research-practice-series/research-practice-series-index/2021-issues/leadership-as-practice-in-early-childhood-education-and-care-settings/

Hazy, J. K., & Uhl-Bien, M. (2015). Towards operationalizing complexity leadership: How generative, administrative and community-building leadership practices enact organizational outcomes. *Leadership, 11*(1), 79–104. https://doi.org/10.1177/1742715013511483

Jorgenson, J., & Steier, F. (2013). Frames, framing, and designed conversational processes: Lessons from the World Cafe. *The Journal of Applied Behavioral Science, 49*(3), 388–405. http://doi.org/10.1177/0021886313484511

Marion, R., & Gonzales, L. D. (2013). *Leadership in education: Organizational theory for the practitioner*. Waveland Press.

Siraj-Blatchford, I., & Manni, L. (2007). *Effective leadership in the early years sector: The ELEYS study*. Institute of Education Press.

Steier, F., Brown, J., & Mesquita da Silva, F. (2015). The World Cafe in action. In H. Bradbury-Huang (Ed.), *The SAGE Handbook of Action Research*. Sage Publications.

The World Café Community Foundation, (2017). *The World Cafe design principles* Retrieved from http://www.theworldcafe.com/key-concepts-resources/design-principles/

Uhl-Bien, M., & Arena, M. (2017). Complexity leadership: Enabling people and organizations for adaptability. *Organizational Dynamics, 46*(1), 9–20. https://doi.org/10.1016/j.orgdyn.2016.12.001

Wilkinson, J., & Kemmis, S. (2014). Practice theory: Viewing leadership as leading. *Educational Philosophy and Theory*, 1–17. https://doi.org/10.1080/00131857.2014.976928

Yin, R. (2012). A (Very) Brief Refresher on the Case Study Method. In R. Yin (Ed.), *Applications of Case Study Research*. Sage Publications.

Index

Pages in *italics* refer to figures and pages in **bold** refer to tables.

Adriano, M. N. 135
Alchin, I. 26
Arena, M. 121
Aubrey, C. 25, 40
Australian early childhood education (ECE) sites 160, **161–162**

Barblett, L. 4, 34
Bellwether Education Partners 93
Bloom, J. 81, 83
Bloom, P. J. 22
Bøe, M. 42, 132, 134
Bolman, L. 24, 36
Brinkerhoff, M. 46
Bronfenbrenner, A. 82
Brownlee, J. 39

Center for the Study of Child Care Employment (CSCCE) 93
Cilliers, P. 83
Coleman, A. 67, 121
complex adaptive systems (CAS) 34, 43, 79, 81–89
complexity leadership theory (CLT) 34, 42–45, *44*, 121, 165
continuous professional development model 91
Contractor, N. 46

Deal, T. 24, 36
Dialogic café method 165–166
dispositions: anticipated growth 61; complexity and shapes pathways 60; contextual literacy 71; ECEC leadership 63–64; 'effective' leadership 74–75; emerging and positional leaders 71–73; equality 73; knowledge, skills and values 57, 64, **65–66**, 67–72; leader and educator 61–63; overview of 57–58; practices of leading and leadership 75; respect 73; stories of becoming and belonging 58–59; valuing others 72
distributed leadership 34, 40–41, 47–50, 128
distributed leadership theory 47, 50
Douglass, A. 22, 26–27
Drucker, P. 24, 36

early childhood education and care (ECEC) 1–3, 34; Asia-Pacific, Australia 89–90; Asia-Pacific, Japan 93–95; complex adaptive systems (CAS) theory 82–89; complexity 80; Eastern Europe, Hungary 96–97; ecological systems theory

Index

82; educational practices 97–98; education complex 87–88, *88*; general systems theory 81; initial teacher and educator preparation 89; knowledge, skills and values 118–121, **119–120**; leading and leadership development 117; North America, United States 92–93; Northern Europe, the Nordic model 90–92; overview 79–80; purpose of leadership 117–118; sites of *86*, 86–87; South America, Chile 95–96

early childhood education (ECE) 2–3, 23, 49, 64, 71, 73, 92, 118, 148–150, 155, 158, 160, 165

Early Childhood Work Environment Survey (ECWES) 131

Early Educator Investment Collaborative (EEIC) 92–93

Early Years Learning Framework 89

Early Years Workforce Strategy 22

Ebrahim, H. B. 62

ECEC leadership: collective leadership 42; command and control leadership 36–37; complexity leadership theory (CLT) 42–45, *44*; conceptualisations of 35–36; distributed leadership 40–41; generative leadership 41–42; the Great Man theory 38; leadership-as-practice 45–51; overview of 34; trait theory 38; transformational leadership 38–39

ECEC organisational theory 83

ecological systems theory 81–82

Effective Leadership in Early Years Study (ELEYS) 23

Effective Provision of Preschool Education (EPPE) 23

Fisher, C. M. 37

the Flag Project 69–70

focus groups 8, 133, 169

Fonsén, E. 140

Froebel, F. 18

general systems theory (GST) 81–83

Gibbs, L. 42, 47

Gonzales, L. 121

Great Man theory 38

Hayes, A. 18

Hazy, J. 121

Heckman, J. 15

Heikka, J. 41

Hills, L. 24

Hognestad, K. 42

Hujala, E. 41

Irvine, S. 21

Jung, J.-H. 38

Kemmis, S. 5, 34, 57, 87–88, *88*, 106

Klevering, N. 26

knowledge, skills and values; *see also* dispositions; contextual literacy 71; dispositions 68; emerging and positional leaders 69, 71; the Flag Project 69–70; reinvigorating practice 70–71; self-perception **65–66**

Kroll, L. 67

leadership-as-practice: contemporary conceptualisations 46; development 47; distributed leadership 48, 50; leadership theories 46–47; strength-based communication 50; theoretical framing 45; transformational leadership 47, 49; undergraduate perspectives 47–51

leadership, ECEC: children's well-being 2–3; common narratives 15–20; complexity of 5; context of leading 19; diverse nature of 20; effective leadership 2, *2*, 20; familiar themes 4; hope and optimism 28; in-depth exploration 6; learning for leading 6; management 27–28; observation

Index

tool **163–164**; organisations cultivation 5–6; origin story 18–19; philosophy 46–50; professionalism and practice 3; shaping leadership 5–6; skills, knowledge and values 5; story of 14–15; studies of 6–8; theories and conceptualisations 4; troubles and challenges 21–27
Leadership for the Disillusioned 117
leadership resilience: advocacy and policy reform 149; commitment and motivation 154–155; complexity 158; family and community engagement 150; focus on 151–152; impetus and diversity in 152–153; inclusion and equity 150; innovative teaching practices 148–149; joy and pride 153–154; professional learning 149; recognition of 148; theme and enduring message 156; thinking ahead 148; troubles and challenges 156
leading change-cultivating leadership 115–117
Leary, M. R. 64

Manni, L. 121
Marion, R. 83, 121
McNae, R. 26
Montessori, M. 18
Moyles, J. 23
Muijs, D. 36

National Association for the Education of Young Children (NAEYC) 92
National Institute for Early Education Research (NIEER) 93
National Professional Qualification for Early Years Leadership (NPQEYL) 130
Neill, C. 46
Nicholson, J. 67
Nicolini, D. 46
Nordic model for ECEC 90–92

organisational and individual needs: advocacy and policy influence 140; child development 140; evolving educational practices 139; meeting diverse needs 139; pedagogical leadership 139–140; regulatory requirements 139
organisations cultivating and shaping leadership: arrangements 107; conversation with leaders 106; cultural-discursive arrangements 108; emergence and development of leadership 121–123, **122**; emerging leaders 114; governance practices, ECEC 115; overview 105–106; professional knowledge 109–113; social-political arrangements 113–114; trust 108–109

Pestalozzi, J. H. 18
Press, F. 18
professional learning: adult learners 135; advocacy 143; alignment with organisational goals 137–138; barriers to leadership growth 128; change management 141; collaboration and networking 137; commitment to lifelong learning 136; culture of continuous learning 126; ethical considerations 138; experience 134; future leaders 132–134; integration of technology 138; leadership and practices of leading 129–132; leadership development 142; learning process 135; mentoring and coaching relationships 138; motivation 135; organisational and individual needs 139–140; orientation to learning 135; overview 126–127; passions and interests 140; personalised plans 136–137; practice relevance 137; principles for 135–138; readiness to learn 134; reflective practice 137;

Index

resource management 138; self-perception 134; spheres of influence 129; 'symbiotic' relationship 128; time 135
Program Administration Scale (PAS) 131

Quinones, G. 62

reflective inquiry 8, 169
Rodd, J. 4, 34
Rosa, E. D. 135
Rothfuss, P. 14

Schneider, M. 81
Sergiovanni, T. 24
Sheerer, M. 22
Sinclair, A. 20, 59–61, 117
single-handed heroism 20, 61
Siraj-Blatchford, I. 121
Somers, M. 81
Soukainen, U. 140
Spillane, J. P. 40
Stamopoulos, E. 4, 34
Stipanovic, S. 27
strength-based communication 50
strength-based leadership 49
structured and semi-structured interviews 168–169
Sullivan, D. 23
survey respondents 168
Sylva, K. 15

Taking Charge of Change (TCC) program 131–132
Tangney, J. P. 64
Teaching and Learning International Survey (TALIS) 115, 132
Training Needs Assessment Survey (TNAS) 131
trait theory 38
transformational leader 38–39, 47, 49
transformational leadership 38–39, 49
troubles and challenges 21–27; diverse conceptualisations 22–24; effective leadership 22–24; professional development 27; uncertain pathways 25–27; workforce retention and supply issues 21–22
Tucker, D. 38

Uhl-Bien, M. 121
United Nations Convention 93

vocational education and training (VET) 89

Waniganayake, M. 4, 27, 34, 60
Wartzman, R. 24, 36
Weisz-Koves, T. 26
World Café 166–168

Zaslow, M. 89

Printed in the United States
by Baker & Taylor Publisher Services